Community Engagement
Step-by-Step ACTION KIT

2nd Edition
Revised & Expanded

By Hildy Gottlieb

Community Engagement
Step-by-Step ACTION KIT

2nd Edition
Revised & Expanded

By Hildy Gottlieb

Production Layout & Design by Dimitri Petropolis
Hand Model: Erin Tierney

Renaissance Press
www.RenaissancePress.net
1-520-321-4433

ISBN: 978-0-9714482-5-4

Published by:

Renaissance Press • *Tucson, Arizona*
4433 E. Broadway Blvd Ste. 202
Tucson, Arizona 85711 U.S.A.

Also by Hildy Gottlieb

Books

- The Pollyanna Principles: Reinventing "Nonprofit Organizations" to Create the Future of Our World

- FriendRaising: Community Engagement Strategies for Boards Who Hate Fundraising but Love Making Friends

- Board Recruitment & Orientation: A Step-by-Step, Common Sense Guide

- Building Support Through Public Speaking: Tips Tools and Secrets Any Leader Can Master

- What Do Funders Want? (And Why Do They Want It?): No Nonsense Insights from Funders Themselves

E-Books

- Crafting Great Sleuthing Questions: The Heart of Community Engagement

- The Most Important Thing Is... Exercises for Determining Your Organization's Core Values

- If I Were a Consultant to the American Red Cross (or to Your Organization!): Simple Things Your Organization Can Learn from the Red Cross's Mistakes

Community Engagement
Step-by-Step ACTION KIT
2nd Edition Revised & Expanded

By Hildy Gottlieb

Table of Contents

Preface

Imagine what your community would look like if everyone was inspired to what is possible. Imagine what your programs would look like if they were built upon the community's wisdom and ideas - if they were sustained by the community's passion.

Welcome to the world of Community Engagement!

Whether you are a direct provider of services, a funder, a resource center - engaging the community in your mission will enhance your ability to make a bigger difference in your community. And the very act of engagement will make the community a better place, all at the same time!

That is the reason we created this Action Kit. We know that once you see how easy it is to engage the community in your work, that you will use Community Engagement in more and more of that work. We know you will find it to be easy, effective, and energizing, all at once. And we know the results will help create the healthy, vibrant community you dream of.

Making Community Engagement Practical
This *Action Kit* is just what it says - a step-by-step guide for creating and implementing your Community Engagement plan.

- The *Action Kit* will provide you with the background for understanding what Community Engagement is and what it can accomplish that other approaches cannot.

- The *Action Kit* will provide you not only with the "how-to" for each step in the engagement process, but the reasoning behind those steps.

- The *Action Kit* includes samples for each step in the process, to help clarify each step as you go.

Using the Action Kit with FriendRaising
As you get deeper into your Community Engagement planning, you will find it helpful to use the *Community Engagement Action Kit* in conjunction with its companion book, *FriendRaising: Community Engagement Strategies for Boards Who Hate Fundraising but Love Making Friends*. The hundred or so strategies in FriendRaising will spark even more ideas for Community Engagement activities to help you accomplish your goals.

It is our hope that as you practice engaging the community in every aspect of your work, that Community Engagement moves from being an "activity you do" to simply "the way you are" - moving from *doing* engagement to *being authentically engaged at the core.*

To that end, we invite you to please share your stories with us. We want the world to know about the amazing things that happen when you knock down the walls between the community you serve and the work you do.

Now get out there, and engage your community!!

With gratitude for the work you do to make your community a healthy, vibrant place to live,

PART 1

Introduction to Community Engagement

What is Community Engagement?

What is Community Engagement?

Imagine what your community would look like if everyone was inspired to what is possible. Imagine what your programs would look like if they were built upon the community's wisdom and ideas - if they were sustained by the community's passion.

Our communities are rich in resources, hiding in plain sight and waiting to be engaged to improve the quality of life of everyone (and everything) living there. Sitting at the top of that list of resources are a community's human resources.

When we engage the people who live in our communities to further the vision, mission and values at the heart of the work of a community benefit organization, everyone becomes energized.

When "Community Engagement" moves beyond a list of activities, however, and becomes a way of being, that energy itself can transform a community.

Along the way, that engagement will build and sustain your programs. But those strong programs are not the goal of such engagement; they are simply a fabulous by-product. The ultimate goal of Community Engagement is just that - an engaged community.

With an engaged community, there is no limit to what is possible.

Community Engagement is Friendship

Community Engagement is the process of building relationships with community members who will work side-by-side with you as an ongoing partner, to make the community a better place to live. Considered from the perspective of that two-way relationship, Community Engagement is the organizational equivalent of friendship.

> My best friend knows me better than I know myself sometimes. She knows my history, my background. She knows what I am passionate about, my dreams. She shares information she thinks will help with my work, and she shares stories she thinks I will enjoy. She asks for my advice about her life, and shares her own advice about my life. The more open and honest I am in my friendship with her, the more joy the relationship brings.

> My best friend will help me out when times are tough, and she gives me some of the best presents I have ever received. And I do the same for her.

That is friendship.

When we are talking about Community Engagement, therefore, we are not using the word Friend as it is commonly used in Community Benefit work - as a euphemism for "donor".

We are not talking about the transactional act of "friendraising" as a precursor to asking someone for money - the watchword that "fundraising is about relationship building," which suggests that we get to know people simply so we can eventually ask them to give dollars to the cause.

And we are not suggesting determining how much value someone has to the organization based on how much money he or she can provide.

Instead Community Engagement is about the same kinds of honest, supportive two-way relationships that make our personal lives strong. Community Engagement sets the stage for building and then sustaining great programs, while simultaneously building and sustaining great communities.

By deeply engaging community members in every aspect of a program, the program will be better able to weather life's storms. Everything you do will be infused with a higher level of energy and effectiveness. That engagement is not just uplifting for your program; it is uplifting for everyone involved.

Just like friendship.

Nemawashi

In western culture, projects are typically proposed, developed, then unveiled. With the culture of rugged individualism in our veins, a project will sink or swim on the merits of the individual group proposing and developing that effort.

Traditional Japanese culture does not exalt the individual as we do in the west - just the opposite. The proverb, "The nail that sticks up gets hammered down" better describes the Japanese cultural views on individualism.

The more important factor in that culture is therefore not glory for the individual who came up with the idea or project, but the success that accompanies a group's embracing that effort.

The concept of Nemawashi goes to the heart of that cultural importance of consensus. Put simply, Nemawashi is the process of laying the groundwork for consensus from the very genesis of an effort, working out the bugs, finding out what the obstacles and barriers will be, learning about alternative approaches. With that groundwork laid ahead of time, when the effort IS ready to be unveiled, it has unanimous support, and is built with the input of many great minds, rather than just one or two. The industrial successes for which the Japanese became known in the latter part of the 20th Century are often credited in great part to the Nemawashi process.

Nemawashi happens informally and quietly. It can look messy to outsiders, as it is non-linear (and if we westerners are anything, it is linear!). It takes a great deal more time in the beginning, but efforts are far more likely to succeed in the long term when that groundwork is done well beforehand.

Community Engagement in Practice

Community Engagement in Practice

When all an organization's efforts are seen through the lens of Community Engagement, the first step in any effort is to ask, *"How could this effort be enhanced by engaging others?"*

If you are thinking about developing a new program, Community Engagement means asking that question before you have done much more than sketch out the idea. Before you've consternated over how to put it all together. Before you've budgeted and planned.

And while Community Engagement is a powerful mechanism for building new programs, the real power comes when Community Engagement - friendship - becomes simply a way of being for your whole organization. Instead of "doing Community Engagement activities," you will find your organization is simply "deeply engaged with your community at all levels."

The benefits of engagement - either as a mechanism or as a way of being - are immediately obvious.

- More wisdom to build upon.
- Not having to be the "expert" but being able to be part of a whole group of "experts."
- Replacing a sense of us-and-them with a sense of shared ownership of that effort.
- Dozens of committed, caring friends, to help build and maintain the effort, advocating for that work in all sorts of ways.
- And ultimately, the benefit of more widespread impact in our communities.

The best way to share how this happens is to show what it looks like when we assume programs will be stronger if they are built by the kind of engagement that simultaneously strengthens our communities.

At the heart of all these efforts is the question noted above - *"How can this effort be enhanced by engaging others?"*

As you practice the work in this Action Kit, however, don't be surprised if that question begins to transform into an even more powerful question:

"What can we accomplish together that none of us can accomplish on our own?"

Engaging Everyone: Building the Diaper Bank

Our first experience with the possibilities inherent in Community Engagement came when we set out to build the world's first Diaper Bank.*

As we began to consider how to build this new entity, we knew we wanted the effort to have long-term impact in changing our community. We wanted it to build on the successes we had created in our annual Diaper Drives. We wanted it to be owned by everyone, as that was the road to changing hearts and minds, and thereby changing our community.

But we had no idea what that meant we needed to do.

As consultants, though, we knew where to find those answers. We listed everyone whose lives had been touched by the annual Diaper Drives we had held as our way of giving back to the community at holiday time. And we set out to do our homework, to find the answers to our questions.

Through a process we have come to call Community Sleuthing**, we met with anyone who would meet with us. We asked them a lot of questions, just like any good sleuth would do. We asked for their ideas, their wisdom, and their experience. We engaged them.

We spoke with philanthropists, social service providers and the actual recipients of the diapers. We met with teachers and students; with people who had donated diapers year after year, and with our congressman.

We met with the people we knew. They connected us to the people they knew.

We asked the same questions of everyone.

> How to build the diaper bank? How to run it?
> How to address the big picture issues of poverty, seniors issues, disability, and everything in between?
> What had they seen work well? What had they seen work horribly?
> Who else should we talk with?

We asked and asked and asked. And through that process of engagement, everything about the way we had thought we were going to build the Diaper Bank changed.

---

* The story of our building the first Diaper Bank is detailed in two of our other books - **The Pollyanna Principles: Reinventing "Nonprofit Organizations" to Create the Future of Our World** and **FriendRaising: Community Engagement Strategies for Boards Who Hate Fundraising but Love Making Friends**.

** The "how-to" of Community Sleuthing - our own version of the Nemawashi process - is described in detail in **FriendRaising: Community Engagement Strategies for Boards Who Hate Fundraising but Love Making Friends**.

The Diaper Bank's Results

Our building the first diaper bank was the natural outgrowth of our consulting firm's annual philanthropic "giving back to the community," beginning in the early 1990's. Having raised hundreds of thousands of diapers in a few short years, by 1999 it was clear that no one was addressing the need for this critical commodity in our community. When we looked online to find how other diaper banks had formed, we found there were no other diaper banks. We were about to build the very first one.

Being consultants, we had the perfect picture in our minds of what the Diaper Bank would look like - a stand-alone program much like our local food bank. We could not have known, though, that through the process of engaging the community, a whole new way of building programs would emerge.

The need for a new approach became more and more clear with every conversation. One by one, community leaders from all walks of life asked, "Do we really need another organization? There is so much duplication already. Yes, we know no one is distributing diapers - but does it have to be a separate organization?"

Those conversations allowed us to explore with all those smart individuals two distinct aspects of what we were about to build.

1. There were aspects of the Diaper Bank that were 100% unique - that no one else was doing. First there was its overarching vision - to create a community where we did not assume crisis and poverty would always be part of life. Second was the Diaper Bank's mission. Obviously no one was collecting and distributing diapers, but neither was anyone telling the stories of all those other organizations as one big story, showing how everything affected everything else.

2. There were aspects of the Diaper Bank that were absolutely duplicative. Others in the community were already doing large parts of the day-to-day work the Diaper Bank would need to do, to accomplish its mission and aim towards its vision - warehousing, case management, transportation - even tax exemption.

These distinctions became clear only through our discussions with our fellow community members. From those conversations, everything changed about our initial assumptions about building the Diaper Bank.

Instead of building a stand-alone, we-do-it-all organization, the Diaper Bank became the collaborative effort of multiple community partners, each doing the piece of the work they were already doing. We shared warehouse space and vehicles; case management and yes, even tax exemption. Through that shared work, the Diaper Bank's role became just two main tasks:

1. Guide the mission and vision - the work no one else was doing
2. Coordinate all the partners to get that work done.

That whole model (which is described in how-to detail in **The Pollyanna Principles**), would never have happened had it not been for our conversations with community members.

In addition, though, many of the individual components of that collaboration were also the result of engagement.

The best example of that effect was the Diaper Bank's fiscal sponsorship. The truth is that while we were engaging in all our sleuthing conversations, we had the paperwork for acquiring the Diaper Bank's own tax exempt status sitting on my desk, waiting to be filled out and sent to the IRS.

As a result of our conversation with a fundraising colleague, however, we were introduced to the CEO of a local hospital foundation. When we asked that CEO for her experience and ideas, she suggested fiscal sponsorship, and further offered the hospital foundation as that fiscal sponsor!

The same sort of "guided serendipity" occurred as we were preparing the Request for Proposals for the warehouse. As we continued engaging people, asking how they might handle the RFP process, most suggested the same likely players - the Food Bank, the Salvation Army.

But one wise soul suggested, "Send the RFP to everyone. You never know who has what." If it were not for our conversation with that individual, we never would have found the perfect warehousing partner. And we would have been back at square one, because in fact, neither the Food Bank nor the Salvation Army had room for the Diaper Bank!

The list of results goes on. From our engagement efforts, we learned more about the issues in our community. We learned how food banking works - the closest thing to what we would be doing. We learned who was already doing what in our community. We were introduced to people it might have otherwise taken eons to get to know, simply because we were not asking for anything more than their wisdom and ideas.

Engaging Another Community to Build a Second Diaper Bank

Given all the wisdom and ideas we gained through our sleuthing activities, we had no idea when we opened the Diaper Bank's doors in 2000 how important that highly engaged approach would be to our next steps. Within only a few months of that opening, the Diaper Bank was receiving an ongoing stream of calls from groups across the nation and around the world, asking how they, too, could start a diaper bank.

Anxious to determine if the shared-resource model could be replicated, to suggest that approach to others who called for advice, we investigated the possibility of building another Diaper Bank in the same collaborative way. That led to our traveling 125 miles up the road from our hometown of Tucson to Phoenix.

The Phoenix metro area is home to approximately 3.5 million people, in a land mass that spreads over more than 1,000 square miles. Engaging individuals in our hometown had been relatively easy. Phoenix, however, is almost four times the size of Tucson, and we knew only a handful of people there.

Using the same approach that had built the Diaper Bank in Tucson, we got to work engaging the individuals we knew in Phoenix. These people were not movers and shakers - a dental consultant, an accountant, a banker, a human resources consultant. However, because we knew that everyone cares about building a strong, healthy community, we knew we would learn a great deal as we began our conversations with the people we knew, asking them to connect us with others, and then with others again, all around that shared vision.

While Tucsonans already knew about the Diaper Drive, in Phoenix, the concept was brand new. In the spirit of the Nemawashi approach to building new programs, we announced nothing until we had engaged dozens and dozens of individuals in conversation. When we did finally announce the effort, we invited those who wanted to participate in building the Phoenix Diaper Bank to a community-wide meeting, thinking that a handful of dedicated individuals would step up to do that work. Imagine our surprise when seventy-five people showed up to help! From that group, fifty volunteers met for a year, putting the infrastructure in place to open the doors to the Valley of the Sun Community Diaper Bank.

In both Tucson and Phoenix, virtually every single person we engaged became a staunch supporter of the Diaper Bank. People shared their ideas, their perspectives, and their contacts. Those contacts then shared their own contacts. What started as "our idea" became theirs.

All these many years later, those same individuals are still engaged. They are still volunteering, still making connections, still donating dollars, and still advocating for the cause.

All that and more was the result of asking for something each of us has in abundance - our ideas, our experience, and our wisdom.

Engaging Doctors: The Cancer Support Group

The Cancer Support Group provides non-medical support to people with cancer - everything from counseling to recreational activities. Despite the success rate of the program, and despite the fact that all its programs are free, the group was having trouble getting doctors to refer their patients.

Here is the approach they had been using for "Physician Outreach":

- Make an appointment
- Tell their story to the doctor
- Ask them to refer their patients
- Leave some literature behind

Things began turning around immediately when instead of being on the nonprofit equivalent of a sales call, the Cancer Support Group began asking and listening. Instead of the one-way effort of "outreach," they began engaging the doctors in real conversations, seeking the doctors' wisdom, rather than doing all the talking and then hoping the doctors would do the right thing.

They did this by asking the questions to which they sorely needed answers:

What would you need to know before you could refer someone to us?

What would put your mind at ease and encourage you to refer your patients? What might stop you from referring someone to us?

Do you have any suggestions for our program that you think might help your own patients - maybe things you aren't seeing anywhere else and have always wished someone would do?

The reward was instantaneous. Doctors not only began referring their patients, but some of those doctors offered to form an advisory panel for the group. All it took was realizing that the doctors shared the vision of the Cancer Support Group. From there it was simply a matter of engaging their wisdom, their ideas, and their experience.

Engaging Bilingual Volunteers: Tax Credit Program

A primarily African American church in a low-income area provided a variety of services to assist people who lived in the surrounding neighborhoods. Those services relied on a large corps of volunteers, almost all of whom were members of the church's congregation. While few of those volunteers spoke Spanish, many of the individuals who needed the group's services spoke only Spanish.

This became critical in the church's Earned Income Tax Credit program, a program that helps low-income families get significant tax refunds. While the group had volunteer accountants to help fill in the tax forms, none spoke Spanish.

Instead of putting the word out that the group needed bilingual volunteer accountants, the group's director changed their intake process. She began asking the clients themselves, "What languages do you speak?"

Sure enough, the group found that some of the clients receiving their services were bilingual in English and Spanish. Now instead of simply being "recipients of the service," they became "volunteer interpreters" who just happened to also be getting their taxes done! They were able to improve the program and turn their "clients" into "partners," simply by engaging the wisdom of the people who were using their services.

Engaging Young People: The Foundation

"Diversity and Inclusion" have become hot topics at many organizations. While a great deal of that focus has been placed on provider organizations, more and more foundations are looking internally, realizing that their own boards and staff often fail to reflect the diverse communities in which they provide funding.

The answer to diversity has, to date, been a prettied-up version of tokenism. I say "prettied-up" because of the unspoken assumption that tokenism for a good cause is somehow ok. But looking around at a board filled with all white faces (for example), noting, "We need faces of color at the table," and then heading out to find one of each of the various races and ethnic groups in town - well, there is no other word for that than tokenism. And if we are going to model the behaviors we want to see in the world, that is not a great start!

The opposite of tokenism is true engagement. When organizations honestly engage the populations they are working to impact, the need for tokenism vanishes.

One of the best examples of this is a small family foundation called Every Voice in Action.

The mission of the Every Voice in Action Foundation is to ignite and support Youth Voice, "infusing the community with the unique perspectives of young people."

Realizing they needed to more deeply engage young people in every aspect of their work, Every Voice in Action developed the Youth Crew - a group of high school and college students that is directly responsible for granting $50,000 annually to youth-related efforts.

Every year, a new Youth Crew learns about philanthropy and learns about the community's issues. The Youth Crew then considers potential focus areas for grants. They write and issue the Request for Proposals, and they review those proposals. Then the Youth Crew makes the final decisions on who gets funding!

No tokenism; true engagement. While the issue of "inclusion" is certainly addressed, the strongest benefit is that the efforts of the Foundation create more impact in the community in the short term (via the project) and in the long term (via the hands-on education and empowerment they are providing to young people).

All this is a result of the decision by Every Voice in Action to be an engaged organization - to always be engaging the wisdom, the ideas and the experience of the population they intend to impact.

Community Engagement: Gardening in the Front Yard

Community Engagement:
Gardening in the Front Yard

Years ago, our Labrador Retriever owned our back yard. She would dig. She would run deep grooves into the grass. Garden after garden fell to Hallie's exploits.

Finally, I dug up a plot next to the driveway. And I planted my vegetables in the front yard.

That was twenty years ago – two houses and another dog ago. And still, my garden is in the front yard.

Tomatoes and okra and basil and zucchini in the summer; lettuce and carrots and peas and broccoli in the desert winter. All in the front yard.

Why the front yard? Because my garden makes friends.

Since moving into my current home, my front yard garden has introduced me to neighbors from many blocks away. Some ask gardening questions. Some put my house on their morning walk route, to see what's new.

And some bring gifts.

That's how I met Earl. My doorbell rang one morning, and there stood a gentle elderly man holding a plastic baggie filled with sunflower seeds. "My wife used to love driving by your house. She always wanted to see what was new. I lost her last month." He handed me the bag of seeds. "These are from her sunflowers."

Every year, from then on, I have planted a wall of sunflowers, swirling along the front sidewalk, in honor of Earl's love for his wife. And of course those giant flowers bring even more new friends.

So why am I sharing this here?

Because planting your garden in the front yard is precisely what Community Engagement is all about.

Community Engagement forms real, honest, engaged relationships between members of the community and your organization's mission and vision.

Community Engagement is not marketing or fundraising or volunteer recruitment, but it will certainly accomplish those things. It will also help you build the most effective programs possible. It will help you further every single one of your goals. And it will help you with the biggest goal of all – building an engaged community (the same goal as my front yard garden).

But here's the real secret – and it is what separates Community Engagement from Marketing and all those other "just for show" efforts: For engagement to work, it has to be honest; it has to be real.

If my front yard were merely a well-manicured, just-for-show row of hedges, no one would stop. No one would introduce themselves. No one would make my house a special part of their day.

My neighbors stroll by because my garden is honest, authentic. In the morning, they find me working. At dinner time, they find us harvesting. There are butterflies and ladybugs. There are finches all over the sunflowers. My neighbors don't just see the final product; they also see the sweat, the compost, the pruning, the digging. I do not have to tell my neighbors I want to engage them - my garden shows them.

And when they walk by with a friend, pointing out this or that, they do so with pride, as if some part of my garden is also theirs. Because, in part, it is.

The difference between gardening in the front yard vs. only showing a perfectly manicured hedge is more than just metaphor. The difference is the degree to which the community feels a part of everything your organization does.

The more your community feels they are a part of your work – the more they can point with pride, feeling that your work is their own as well – the more effective your mission will be, in every single way. And the more every part of your work will be contributing to building a more engaged community overall.

PART 2

Creating Your Community Engagement Plan

Creating Your Community Engagement Plan

As you begin to integrate Community Engagement into your organization's efforts, the following will be the basic planning steps to help guide that plan.

Following this outline, you will find worksheets to help you think through the Community Engagement opportunities available to your organization right now. Each of those forms will begin with a sample. Then the following pages are blank, so you can print as many as you need, to do your own planning work.

As you work through your Community Engagement Plan, we know you will be surprised at how many lives your organization is already touching - folks you can begin to engage at all levels of your work.

Step 1:
Focus on the Community's Potential
> The people in your community all have one thing in common; they all want to live in a place that is healthy, vibrant, resilient. Engaging with the community from that visionary context ensures you are starting the conversation on a note of agreement and enthusiasm.

Step 2:
Determine the Goals of the Plan
> Community Engagement is not a separate activity, but an approach to accomplishing all your organization's work. Therefore, the goals of your Community Engagement Plan will be the Community Engagement needs from all your organization's other plans. As you look at the goals for all your organization's plans, how could Community Engagement help further each of those goals?

Step 3:
Who to Engage?
> For each of those goals, determine who in your community needs to be engaged to ensure that goal can be achieved. You might start by listing broad categories of the types of people you want to get to know for each of those goals (for example, "teachers"). Then once those categories are listed, name names to attach to those categories (for example, "Mr. Cajero, Mrs. Smith"). You cannot engage with a category; for real engagement, you need a live human being.

Step 4:
Develop Engagement Strategies for Those Individuals You Already Know

Determine who on that list you already know. Then, using Community Engagement activities such as those found in **FriendRaising***, determine how you will approach them, and then how you might engage them. It could be through group activities, or one-on-one activities, depending on who you are approaching.

Step 5:
Develop Engagement Strategies for Those Individuals You DO NOT Already Know

Determine who is left on the list - folks you have yet to meet. Using Community Engagement activities such as those found in **FriendRaising***, determine how you will approach them, and then how you might engage them. Again, it could be through group activities, or one-on-one activities, depending on who you are approaching.

Step 6:
Prioritize those Activities

There are only so many hours in a day, and only so many people to help implement this plan. You will therefore need to prioritize, determining which of those activities is most likely to accomplish what you need to accomplish, and then focusing on those. Be objective as you weigh the activities against each other. Do what will get you the best results.

Step 7:
Create an Implementation Plan

Determine what steps you will take to implement each activity you choose. Who will do what, and when?

Step 8:
Monitor Your Progress

Get out there, and do the work. And then monitor your progress. A plan is most effective when it is monitored and adjusted along the way.

Step 9:
Maintain those Relationships

Because Community Engagement is about building relationships, the single most important step in every one of the activities in your plan will be what happens when that activity is done. Build follow-up into your plans for maximum effectiveness.

* The reason we recommend FriendRaising and not some other book of this type is that there is no other book of this type. We wrote FriendRaising in the first place because no one else had done so!

<u>Step 1:</u> Focus on the Community's Potential

If you met someone at a party, and they immediately began talking nonstop about themselves - and then moved the conversation to how you could help them get what they want... how long would it take you to find any excuse to get away?

The same holds true in Community Engagement. If engagement is about building authentic two-way relationships, conversations cannot solely be about what your organization wants from the relationship. The conversation must truly be about what you can accomplish together - the difference you want to make in the community you both care about.

Planning for establishing those relationships will therefore begin with that as the very first step in the plan - clarifying what you want for your community, not for your organization.

Before you can engage others in your efforts, then, Step 1 is about being clear within your own work. What is the ultimate goal of that work?

The following questions are intended as prompts for discussion among your board and staff. Once you have explored the answers, and can clearly articulate the difference you intend to make in your community, you will have created the context for beginning every engagement conversation you have from this point forward.

- As we consider our mission, what would 100% success look like in our community?
- What is the biggest difference your organization could make for your community? What would that difference look like? For whom? Whose lives would be different? Describe what that difference would look like for them.
- Fill in the blank:

    As a result of the work our organization does, our community will be _____.

    (or)

    our community will have _____.

    From there, you might even craft a statement that says,

    Our vision is a community where _____.

Step 2: Determine the goals of the plan

Community Engagement is not a separate activity, but an approach to accomplishing all your organization's work - a way of being, rather than simply a task to do. Therefore, the goals of your Community Engagement Plan will be the Community Engagement needs from all your organization's other plans. As you look at the goals for all your organization's plans, how could Community Engagement help further each of those goals?

Starting with your Community Impact Plan, how could Community Engagement help further this year's goals? If you are seeking to create significant impact in your community, you obviously cannot accomplish that without deep engagement with a wide variety of community members. So look at each of the goals in your Community Impact Plan, and discuss how Community Engagement can help further those goals. The sample on page 37 may help as a thought-starter.

As you move to your Organizational Wellness Plan, you may have many goals - perhaps two or three per functional area of the organization. Each of those many goals may be furthered by Community Engagement. The samples on page 38 may assist as a guide.

Lastly, as you look at any other plans - from Program Development to other plans - you will do the same thing, checking to see how each goal can be furthered by engaging your community. The sample on page 40 may guide you in that area.

Community Impact Goals

How can Community Engagement Further Our Goals?

Sample Goal: Learn more about what other organizations are doing to further our issues.

How can Community Engagement further that goal?

1) Engaging other organizations doing similar work as us, we can learn what they are doing re: big-picture issues, and we can share our own thoughts with them

2) Engaging university professors, they may have info about organizations doing innovative work, while they would also learn about our own work

3) Engaging local policy makers, they may have info about organizations doing similar work at the policy level, while they would also learn about our own work

---

Goal # ___ :

How can Community Engagement further that goal?

1)

2)

3)

Goal # ___ :

How can Community Engagement further that goal?

1)

2)

3)

Goal # ___ :

How can Community Engagement further that goal?

1)

2)

3)

★ *Print multiple copies of this worksheet to be sure you address all your plan's goals.*

Organizational Wellness Goals
How can Community Engagement Further Our Goals?

Sample Goal 1: Personnel Plan: Create a Succession Plan for the ED

How can Community Engagement further that goal?

1) Engaging with other organizations, we can learn what they have done / what has worked well / not worked, and they can learn from us.

2) Engaging former EDs, we can learn what they feel might have worked better

Sample Goal 2: Facilities Plan: Create an Annual Safety Plan

How can Community Engagement further that goal?

1) Engaging the Police Department, we could receive a safety review / get crime prevention input, while they learn more about our program

2) Engaging Fire Safety Officials, we could receive a safety review and get their fire safety ideas, while they learn more about our program

3) Engaging other organizations, we could learn about their own safety plans, and they could learn from what we are learning from others!

Goal # ___ :

How can Community Engagement further that goal?

1)

2)

3)

Goal # ___ :

How can Community Engagement further that goal?

1)

2)

3)

Organizational Wellness Plan - Goals (continued)

Goal # ___ :

How can Community Engagement further that goal?

1)

2)

3)

Goal # ___ :

How can Community Engagement further that goal?

1)

2)

3)

Goal # ___ :

How can Community Engagement further that goal?

1)

2)

3)

Goal # ___ :

How can Community Engagement further that goal?

1)

2)

3)

★ *Print multiple copies of this worksheet to be sure you address all your plan's goals.*

Other Plans: Goals
How can Community Engagement Further Our Goals?

List the goals for any other plans your organization will be implementing this year, per the sample below.

Sample Plan: New Program Development

Sample Goal: Research other similar programs to determine best path for our program

How can Community Engagement further that goal?

1) Engaging other organizations in our community, we can learn who else is doing work on this. We will learn about their programs, and find potential partners while they learn from what we are finding.

2) Engaging foundations, we can learn about similar programs and perhaps make connections with folks running those programs, to learn more - all while funders are learning about our program.

Plan:

Goal # ____ :

How can Community Engagement further that goal?

1)

2)

3)

Plan:

Goal # ____ :

How can Community Engagement further that goal?

1)

2)

3)

Plan:

Goal # ____ :

How can Community Engagement further that goal?

1)

2)

3)

★ *Print multiple copies of this worksheet to be sure you address all your plan's goals.*

Other Plans: Goals (continued)
How can Community Engagement Further Our Goals?

Goal # ___ :

How can Community Engagement further that goal?

1)

2)

3)

Goal # ___ :

How can Community Engagement further that goal?

1)

2)

3)

Goal # ___ :

How can Community Engagement further that goal?

1)

2)

3)

Goal # ___ :

How can Community Engagement further that goal?

1)

2)

3)

★ *Print multiple copies of this worksheet to be sure you address all your plan's goals.*

<u>Step 3:</u> Who to Engage?

You can already see that each of your organization's goals carries a myriad of opportunities to engage the community in a very real way. For Step 3, examine each of those Community Engagement opportunities, and determine who in your community needs to be engaged to ensure your organization's goals can be achieved. You might start by listing broad categories of the types of people you want to get to know for each of those goals. Then once those categories are listed, name names to attach to those categories. You cannot engage with a category; for real engagement, you need a live human being.

Note: Don't just list the people you know. It is important to note everyone you will need to engage with, to optimize your success. Steps 4 & 5 will break down this list into those you know and those you do not yet know. For now, just list the people who would be logical to engage in your work.

Use the format on page 43 for EACH Community Engagement opportunity noted in Step 2. With all your organization's goals, and all your organization's opportunities, this will require many sheets.

A Word About Engaging Other Organizations
You can see from some of the samples that we encourage you to engage other organizations who are doing similar work as you.

> If your goal is intended to directly impact the community - whether that is to build a new program, or attack a new community issue, etc. - it is critical to add to your "list of people to engage" the folks at similar organizations in town, as they care about the same things as you.

The individuals working and volunteering at those organizations are likely thinking about the very issues you are trying to address, and you will be able to accomplish so much more together than alone. So while you are out there contacting users of your service or patrons of your theater; funders and donors; city council members and regular citizens, start engaging your "competition" in that work as well. (And as you have those conversations, don't forget to talk not only with EDs and board members, but program managers, case workers - the folks who have hands-on experience with what is and is not working!)

While you may be nervous the first time you have one of these conversations, you will soon learn the secret to Community Engagement:

> Conversations with people who care about what you care about are the most energizing conversations you can have.

Who to Engage

For each opportunity, name the categories / groups of people to engage, and then name the individuals who fit that category.

SAMPLE Community Engagement Opportunity from Step 2:

Community Impact Goal #1 - Learn About Other Organizations' Work

SAMPLE Category 1:   Other organizations

Name individual people who fit that category:

1) Susan Smith, Exec Director, ABC Group
2) Juanita Perez, Board Member, XYZ Agency
3) John Costanza, Program Director, The Good Group
4) Sally Ann Jenson, Exec Director, Always Excel

SAMPLE Category 2:   Professors at Local University

Name individual people who fit that category:

1) Dr. Ann Walberg, College of Nursing
2) Professor Greenbaum, School of Social Work
3) Professor Steven Ramirez, School of Social Work
4) Dr. Jonathan Pierce, College of Medicine

SAMPLE Category 3:   Policy Makers

Name individual people who fit that category:

1) City Council Member Scott
2) City Council Member Addison
3) School Board Member Ana Lewis
4) State Representative Juanita Cox

Who to Engage

For each opportunity, name the categories / groups of people to engage, and then name the individuals who fit that category.

Community Engagement Opportunity from Step 2:

Category # ____:

Name individual people who fit that category:

1)

2)

3)

4)

Category # ____:

Name individual people who fit that category:

1)

2)

3)

4)

Category # ____:

Name individual people who fit that category:

1)

2)

3)

4)

Category # ____:

Name individual people who fit that category:

1)

2)

3)

4)

★ *Print multiple copies of this worksheet to be sure you address all your plan's goals.*

Who to Engage (continued)

For each opportunity, name the categories / groups of people to engage, and then name the individuals who fit that category.

Community Engagement Opportunity from Step 2:

Category # ____ :

Name individual people who fit that category:
1)
2)
3)
4)

Category # ____ :

Name individual people who fit that category:
1)
2)
3)
4)

Category # ____ :

Name individual people who fit that category:
1)
2)
3)
4)

Category # ____ :

Name individual people who fit that category:
1)
2)
3)
4)

★ *Print multiple copies of this worksheet to be sure you address all your plan's goals.*

<u>Step 4:</u> Develop Engagement Strategies for Those Individuals You Already Know

From Steps 2 and 3, determine who on those lists you already know. Then, using Community Engagement activities such as those found in **FriendRaising**, determine how you will approach them, and then how you might engage those people. These strategies might be group activities, or one-on-one activities, depending on who you are approaching.

Whatever strategies you choose, there is one key to engagement that will make all those strategies more effective. And that is to focus the back and forth on real exchange, rather than simply telling your story - all within the community context you established in Step 1.

With all the marketing classes folks in the Community Benefit Sector have taken, we have gotten pretty good at telling our stories. We have learned to create our 30-second elevator speech, and to create a mission statement with zing. We have become expert at telling how amazing our work is, using examples of how our work has benefitted those who use our services or attend our performances. We may wish we could do it better, but all in all, we are pretty well trained in telling our story - a big part of marketing.

When it comes to Community Engagement activities, however, the point is not to "tell your story," but rather to engage that other person or group of people in a real relationship. And the most effective way to truly engage is not to tell, but to ask.

It may take some time to learn the art of asking, after so many years of telling. But the goal of all the strategies you will list in Steps 4 and 5 will be true, honest engagement - the kind of interaction that acknowledges the value in the person we are engaging. As you actually go out and do these strategies, then, remember this: **Questions are the key to engagement.**

- What do you think about the issues we are addressing?
- What approaches have you seen taken regarding this issue?
- How do you think we might make our programs more accessible, so more folks can benefit?
- Can you think of other programs in town we should be talking with, to see how we might work together?
- And etc.

Two-way engagement is about building real relationships - valuing each other's caring, each other's wisdom, each other's experience. And the only way to find out how deep that caring, wisdom and experience go is to ask.

So as you list the strategies in Steps 4 and 5, consider what opportunities those strategies will provide for building those real relationships. That thinking will help you as you get into Step 6 - Prioritizing. And it will help you determine the success of your efforts.

Strategies for Engaging Individuals You Already Know

SAMPLE Category of People to Engage: Other Organizations

SAMPLE Strategies We Want to Try:

1) Lunch with EDs / Board Members (See Strategy #9 in FriendRaising)

2) Traveling Board Meetings (See Strategy #78 in FriendRaising)

3) Community Sleuthing (See Strategy #10 in FriendRaising)

4) Tours (See Strategy #11 in FriendRaising)

Category of People to Engage:

Strategies We Want to Try:

1)

2)

3)

4)

Category of People to Engage:

Strategies We Want to Try:

1)

2)

3)

4)

Category of People to Engage:

Strategies We Want to Try:

1)

2)

3)

4)

★ *Print multiple copies of this worksheet to be sure you address all your plan's goals.*

<u>Step 5:</u> Develop Engagement Strategies for Those Individuals You DO NOT Already Know

Now that you have determined how you might engage the people you already know, it is time to focus on the folks who are left on your list from Step 3 - those people you have yet to meet. Using Community Engagement activities such as those found in **FriendRaising**, determine how you will approach them, and then how you might engage them. Again, it could be through group activities, or one-on-one activities, depending on who you are approaching.

As you did in Step 4, consider how your strategies could create opportunities for building real relationships. The more opportunity to engage in real dialogue and ask questions, the better your chances for building those relationships.

A Word About Public Speaking and Public Writing

When it comes to engaging individuals you do not already know, some of the strategies in **FriendRaising** refer to public speaking and public writing. When we teach Community Engagement in workshops, a question that often arises is therefore, "How do speaking and writing fit with building real relationships?"

Speaking and writing can indeed be engaging, if you focus on asking questions. A speech can ask an audience to consider scenarios, asking, "What would you do?" The speaker might ask the audience to consider, "Did X ever happen to you? How did you respond? What allowed you to pull through?"

Depending on the group, you can ask rhetorically or you can really seek an answer. Asking rhetorically, you might suggest a question as something to consider, perhaps allowing the audience a bit of time to think about their answer. If it is possible to ask the question in a way that elicits actual responses, though, you will find that asking questions is a great way to engage the whole audience.

Whether you do so by seeking responses to questions you ask the whole group, or by having audience members pair up for a few minutes, to ask a question of each other, the group will indeed be engaged.

A written piece can also ask questions, giving readers a way to engage themselves in the answers. Depending on the format, you can ask readers to email you with their responses and ideas. Or if the piece will be published online, you can end the piece with a question, engaging dialogue in the comments section.

Regardless of the strategies you use, the more you consider how you will create opportunities to ask questions, the more you will see the power those questions have for engaging others in real relationships.

Engagement Strategies for Engaging Those People You DO NOT Already Know

SAMPLE Category of People to Engage: | Policy Makers

SAMPLE Strategies We Want to Try:

1) Meet with Them (See Strategy #39 in FriendRaising)

2) Barn Raising (See Strategy #23 in FriendRaising)

3) Community Sleuthing (See Strategy #10 in FriendRaising)

4) Send an Article We've Had Published (See Strategy #33 in FriendRaising)

Category of People to Engage:

Strategies We Want to Try:

1)

2)

3)

4)

Category of People to Engage:

Strategies We Want to Try:

1)

2)

3)

4)

Category of People to Engage:

Strategies We Want to Try:

1)

2)

3)

4)

★ *Print multiple copies of this worksheet to be sure you address all your plan's goals.*

Step 6: Prioritizing Your Plan - The Magic Matrix

Step 6 is where your organization will take that huge list of possible approaches, and you will determine which will be the most effective at accomplishing your goals. With limited hours in the day, you will want to be certain to choose the most effective strategies possible!

In our experience, far too many organizations make decisions in ways that are not the most effective. We have seen:

- Organizations who make decisions by deferring to a strong board member or ED, even when your gut instinct says this may not be the best choice.
- Organizations who base their decisions on what other organizations do - a keeping up with the Jones's approach.
- Organizations who make decisions in a vacuum - asking, "Should we do this - yes or no?" instead of asking, "Which activity should we choose - this? Or this? Or this?"

That is why for Step 6 - prioritizing and choosing strategies - we encourage the use of objective measures for making those decisions. And the easiest tool for that is what we have come to call the Magic Matrix.

The Magic Matrix encourages decision-making and prioritizing based on objective criteria that will further your organization's mission and its Community Engagement goals. The focus of the Magic Matrix is the opportunity cost of your decisions - "If we choose this activity, we may not be able to do this other one - and the other one actually makes more sense for our goals!" It is intended to encourage broad thinking as you determine which options will be best for both the long term and short term benefit of the work you are doing.

The questions posed by the Magic Matrix cover a broad variety of issues related to your FriendRaising / Community Engagement efforts:

★ **Are we focusing on real friends, or are we still calling folks "friends" but really intending just to ask them to become donors?** By reading the materials in this kit, you know that the purpose of Community Engagement planning is to build an army of real friends, rather than simply labeling our donors as "friends." However, we also know that old habits die hard. The questions in the Magic Matrix therefore ask you to look honestly at your motivations. Will your efforts help you seek real friends - the kind who will help you achieve your organization's goals beyond just their cash donations? Are you seeking to engage the wisdom and experience and other gifts your community has to offer? The Magic Matrix helps you prioritize by reminding you of the real purpose of engaging the community - an engaged community!

★ **Are you focused on results, or are you confusing "actions" with "results?" Are you counting what counts?** Because our organizations have been so trained to "get out there and tell our story," it is sometimes hard to remember that telling our story is not the end goal of our Community Engagement activities. The point of these efforts is what happens *after* we tell our story. It is the difference between thinking, "If we speak in front of 100 people, that is 100 people who will know about us!" vs. asking, "How many of those people will take action based on our talk?" Depending on the group you are addressing, it may be 10% of the attendees, or every single person in the room. The Magic Matrix will encourage you to focus on the result (the 10 people who come up afterwards) rather than the action (speak to 100 people).

★ **At what stage of development is your organization, and how will that affect your decisions?** Different organizations are at different stages in their development, which will affect which results matter most. Younger organizations often need direct results faster than more mature organizations. A more mature organization often has the luxury of planting the seeds for longer term results. That is why we leave it to you to determine which outcomes are the 1's, 2's and 3's in your ranking system.

Magic Matrix™
for Community Engagement

STRATEGIES

1) How many engaged friends might this effort raise?
1 = Few 3 = Many

2) How quickly will this new friend feel connected?
1 = Will take time 3 = Immediately

3) How much cash investment will this effort require?
1 = High cash needs 3 = Low cash needs

4) How work intensive is this effort?
1 = VERY 3 = Not at all

5) Could this effort accomplish more than one of our goals at once?
1 = No 3 = Yes

6) Will this effort create a path to ongoing relationship, or is this really just an Ask?
1 = Just an Ask 3 = Builds relationships

7) Can this effort be executed immediately or will it require prep time / planning?
1 = Will take time 3 = Immediately

8) How much opportunity does this effort give our prospective friend(s) to share their wisdom?
1 = No shared wisdom 3 = Shares wisdom

9) Will this activity create competition with others doing similar work?
1 = Yes 3 = No

10) How dependent is this effort on decisions made by others? Others will make decision
1 = Others will make decision 3 = You make decision

TOTAL

DATE ———

PAGE ———

Instructions for Using the Magic Matrix

1) In the left-hand column, list the Community Engagement strategies you are considering. If you need to use more than one sheet, do so.

2) Across the top you will find a number of objective criteria we have seen organizations grapple with in their decision-making. The blank space is for you to add any specific criteria that may be important to your organization, that we have not included. What objective criteria do you want to base your decisions upon as you choose which strategies to use?

3) If there are criteria we HAVE included, that are NOT important to your organization, disregard them and replace them with your own. If the matrix is not individualized for your own organization's needs, it will not be the best tool it can be for you.

4) For each idea you list in the first column, provide a ranking for each of the decision-making criteria. If the idea is terrific in any given category, it will receive a 3. If it is bad, it will receive a 1. And obviously, the 2's will be those that are neither great nor really bad.

5) If there is discussion that led to the decision to make something a 1 vs. a 3, or a 2 vs. a 1, note that discussion, as shown on the sample on Page 58. You will be happy you have the reasoning behind that choice when you look at the matrix 6 months from now and wonder," Why did we give that a 3? It is clearly a 1!"

6) Add up the rankings in the "Total" space provided. It should be easy to see which are getting the most points vs. those ideas that are less likely to provide the results that are important to your organization.

7) Decision-making: The simplest way to decide which ideas to move forward on is to choose a cut-off ranking, and to go with any idea that falls above that ranking. You might, for example, choose a 75% mark - that if the highest score an idea could get would be a 30, that you will not go with anything at or below 22. (In our sample, that would eliminate "Speaking at Churches" and the "Gala with Slide Show.") There is no magic cut-off number for success - no right or wrong. Your decisions will depend on how your own matrix rankings have come out, based on your own individual needs.

Regardless of what cut-off you choose, by focusing on the highest ranking ideas, you will be working towards the most effective Community Engagement efforts for your organization - based NOT on the emotional "But I really love that event," but on the objective criteria you have chosen.

8) Further decision-making rankings can be done easily with the Magic Matrix. For example, if one criteria is overwhelmingly important to you, you might decide that you will FURTHER rank the highest scores, to choose only those that have a 3 in that category.

Again, looking at the sample on page 58, our first cut (which we had decided, for our group, would include anything above 22) meant we would choose between the Breakfast Campaign, the Focus Group, and the Volunteer Events. Further ranking could be based on workload, or on the number of friends netted, as follows:

- Workload: If you are severely understaffed and can only do things that require very little staff time, you might decide you will eliminate any idea that doesn't rank a 3 in the "work intensive" category.

  Of those ideas that ranked over 22 in our sample, that would place the Breakfast Campaign at the top of the list.

- Net the Most Friends: If you wanted to choose only those high ranking ideas that would net the most engaged friends, you might decide to choose the highest ranking idea that also has a 3 in the "How many engaged friends?" category.

  Of those ideas that ranked over 22 in our sample, this would focus your energy on Volunteer Events.

Note: It is important to remember that this step is a narrowing down step. You will have already decided that your first cut of ideas will include only those whose rankings **total** over a certain amount, and that the rest just do not measure up in the aggregate. This is not the time to bring back ideas that were tossed out in that first cut. It is only a further ranking of the group that is already in the "yes" list - a narrowing down of that first tier to fit your specific needs.

Magic Matrix Criteria Guide

Note: As you consider the rankings we have assigned to the criteria, you may disagree with what we have considered to be "positive" or "negative" attributes. If that is the case, re-assign the 3 to represent whichever choice would be most favorable for your group, and the 1 to represent the least favorable choice.

1) How many engaged friends might this effort raise?

Over the period you will be measuring, how many real engaged friends will this raise? This question immediately focuses you on real results. It helps you differentiate between the action you will take (for example, "getting the word out so that many people know about us") and the goal of that action - finding real engaged friends as a result of getting the word out.

Some efforts may actually engage many people at once. Other efforts may address many people, but truly engage relatively few. And still other efforts may be slow-and-steady, engaging an individual at a time.

For this question, then, consider your measurement period (typically 1 year), and ask, "How many new engaged friends will come from this effort in that year?" Whether you are planning on executing this effort once a month on an ongoing basis forever; whether it will be a one-time or annual event - count up how many engaged friends might result from this effort by the end of the year. Your response will range from a 3 (many friends) to a 1 (few friends).

2) How quickly will this new friend feel connected?

Will the effort require that there be follow-up steps before this friend will understand how he/she can best fit in and assist? Or is it likely, after this one effort, that your new friend will feel immediately connected and able to pitch in? Your response will range from a 3 (quick connection) to a 1 (will take time).

3) How much cash investment will this effort require?

Some strategies for Community Engagement are virtually cost free (for example, taking someone on a tour). Other efforts may cost some money, but not a lot - perhaps going to breakfast. While others may mean a more concerted cash outlay, including staff time (remember, staff time is money!), the expense of printing materials, or catering an event. We have assigned a 3 to those efforts that are the least costly, and a 1 to those that are most costly.

4) How work intensive is this effort?

Will this effort require lots of staff time and volunteer time? Or is it easy to do? We have assigned a 3 to those efforts that require little more than one person picking up the phone, and a 1 to those efforts that are anticipated to require a lot of work to accomplish.

Magic Matrix Criteria Guide - *continued*

5) Could this effort accomplish more than one of our goals at once?

Step 2 of the planning process makes it clear that Community Engagement can help further many of your organization's goals. And given how little time any of us has to waste, the best activities will be those that can help us accomplish more than one goal at once. How many of your goals will this effort help to address? If it can accomplish a great deal, all with just one activity, rank it a 3. If it really will only accomplish one or two of your many goals, give it a 1.

6) Will this effort create a path to ongoing relationship, or is this really just an Ask?

If you need something, and you are connecting to someone who can provide that - a donor, an in-kind supporter, etc. - are you beginning the relationship with the intent of that Ask? Do you have a plan for extending the relationship beyond asking, and into a deep engagement with your mission, if not before you get the thing you need right now, then after, and into forever? Your response will range from a 3 (builds relationships) to a 1 (just an Ask).

7) Can this effort be executed immediately or will it require prep time / planning?

How soon can we get started? Is this something we will need planning time and lead time to execute, or can we start immediately? A lunch appointment might be able to happen virtually instantly, while an event will require more lead time and planning. Your response will range from a 3 (can happen immediately) to a 1 (will require lead time / planning time).

8) How much opportunity does this effort give our prospective friend(s) to share their wisdom?

The wealthiest person in the world has more wisdom than he has money. And when we engage people at the level of their wisdom, they feel differently about us than when we simply show we value them for the dollar amount of the monetary gifts they share. Ask for someone's money, and they are either happy or begrudging to share it. Ask for someone's wisdom, and we touch their hearts. We are showing we value them for who they are and what they value, what they hope to leave behind after they are gone - the essence of who they are at their core. Your response will range from a 3 (creates the opportunity to share wisdom) to a 1 (no opportunity for shared wisdom).

Magic Matrix Criteria Guide - *continued*

9) Will this activity create competition with others doing similar work?

Some of the activities you choose may create competition with those who are also dedicated to creating the kinds of changes you want to see in your community - other organizations doing similar work. Will this effort open the door to cooperation, or could it be seen as the road to competition? (And are there ways, as you consider developing this project, to change the effort just a bit, to make it less competitive, more open to engaging those like-minded souls?) Your response will range from a 3 (cooperative) to a 1 (competitive).

10) How dependent is this effort on decisions made by others?

To what degree will this event rely on decisions made by someone other than those doing the work? For example, the ultimate decision about whether or not you will be able to engage an individual in a sleuthing conversation will involve the board member making the call, and the person on the other end of the phone. However, the ultimate decision about whether or not a television appearance might happen will rely on decisions outside the influence of your organization. We have assigned a 3 to those decisions that your organization can make relatively autonomously, and a 1 to those decisions that will almost exclusively be made outside your control.

A NOTE about the Sample on Page 58

You may wonder why we have included the "Gala with Slide Show" among our sample activities. Here is why: When we have applied the criteria of our other Magic Matrix - the Magic Matrix for Resource Development - to events such as a gala or golf tournament, those events never measure up against other more effective means of developing resources. It is at that time that the group will often tell us, "Yes, but it's not just a fundraiser - it's a FRIEND raiser." We have therefore included that event in this sample to prove, once and for all, that with very rare exception, for the vast majority of organizations, events such as galas and golf tournaments are not only bottom tier for raising money, they are also bottom tier for raising friends and engaging our communities in our work.

Magic Matrix™ for Community Engagement

DATE ———   PAGE ———

Strategies	1) How many engaged friends might this effort raise? 1 = Few 3 = Many	2) How quickly will this new friend feel connected? 1 = Will take time 3 = Immediately	3) How much cash investment will this effort require? 1 = High cash needs 3 = Low cash needs	4) How work intensive is this effort? 1 = VERY 3 = Not at all	5) Could this effort accomplish more than one of our goals at once? 1 = No 3 = Yes	6) Will this effort create a path to ongoing relationship or is this really just an Ask? 1 = Just an Ask 3 = Builds relationships	7) Can this effort be executed immediately or will it require prep time / planning? 1 = Will take time 3 = Immediately	8) How much opportunity does this effort give our prospective friend(s) to share their wisdom? 1 = No shared wisdom 3 = Shares wisdom	9) Will this activity create competition with others doing similar work? 1 = Yes 3 = No	10) How dependent is this effort on decisions made by others? 1 = Others will make decision 3 = You make decision	TOTAL
BREAKFAST CAMPAIGN	1	3	3	3	3	3	3	3	3 INVITE THEM!	3	28
FOCUS GROUPS	2	3	3	2	3	3	1	3	3 INVITE THEM!	3	26
VOLUNTEER EVENTS	3	2	2	1	3	3	1	2	3 INVITE THEM!	3	23
SPEAKING AT CHURCHES	3	2	3	3	3	2	2	1	2	1	22
GALA WITH A SLIDE SHOW	500 ATTEND—10% BECOME FRIENDS? 2	2	1	1	1	1	1	1	1	SPONSORS, PRESENTERS, ETC. 2	13

Step 7: Implementation Planning

No plan is complete without details regarding who will do what, when, and if funds need to be allocated, how much (and how those funds will be obtained!). That is the heart of implementation planning.

Implementation planning does not require special software or any other fancy tools. A desk-top calendar and sticky-notes are all you need to ensure that the plan is assigned, and that those assignments can be monitored.

Implementation Planning Supplies

1: Set-up

The easiest way to set up the calendar is to rip all 12 months off the pad. Lay out those pages 3 months at a time, going vertically - January, February and March. Then April, May and June. And etc. When you are done, you should have 4 long, taped-together "pages" of 3 months apiece, representing a quarter of the year at a time.

2: Work Backwards to Determine Tasks

While goals such as "implement a monthly newsletter to be received via postal mail" or "re-work the website" may seem large and looming, it is easy to plan out the tasks involved in any goal by working backwards from the final result.

The easiest way to show how to do this is to use an example we are all familiar with: Making sure we arrive at the airport in time to catch a plane. We have all had the experience of setting our alarm clocks by working backwards, as follows:

- If the plane leaves at 9am, I will need to be at the airport at 7am.

- To be at the airport at 7am, I need to leave the house by 6:30.

- I still have about an hour of packing to do, so I must begin packing no later than 5:30.

- I have to shower and feed the dog - that's about ½ hour - so I will have to get up at 5am.

We have all done this. We do it for figuring out what to do when dinner needs to be served at a particular time, or for any other time-critical event. We work backwards all the time. And we do it naturally.

Taped-together Quarter

So that is exactly what you will do for both determining and calendaring all the necessary tasks for implementing your Community Engagement activities!

The following example will use a simple mailing - an annual letter from the board - to show how to work backwards to identify each and every bite-sized task required to bring this goal to fruition. At each point, you can see that the question asked was, "What has to happen before we are ready to do this step?"

Activity: Board letter mailing

Steps (working backwards from the goal):

11   Letter goes to Post Office

10   Stuff / seal / add postage

9   Board members write personal notes to those they know

8   Print addresses on envelopes

7   Make sure mailing list is complete / updated

6   Letter returns from printer

5   Purchase postage (and get sacks from Post Office for transporting the mailing)

4   Send letter to printer (lots of photos - want it professionally printed)

3   Purchase envelopes

2   Write letter

1   Determine what to focus on in letter

Working backwards, determine how long each task will take, to be sure to allow enough time to meet your deadline.

Working backwards makes it easier to ensure no steps are missed. The question at each step will be, "What has to happen before this can take place?"

As you brainstorm these bite-sized tasks, write each task on its own sticky note. You will be using those sticky notes to create your calendar. For now, you may want to temporarily just put them in a loose general order - not by date, just loosely arranged. (You will rearrange these notes more accurately as part of the next step.) The most important part of this step, though, is simply to be sure that there is a sticky note for every part of every task someone mentions, even if that task is as simple as, "Go to post office and buy stamps."

3: Arranging the Calendar

Now that you have identified all the steps that must occur to get the job done, and you have written each task on its own sticky note, it is time to arrange those notes on the calendar. Again, work backwards - start with the deadline for the final task, and place that sticky note on that deadline date. Then, as you look at the next-to-last task (in our example, the task of **"Stuffing / Sealing / Adding postage"**), you will ask, "How long will it take to complete that task?" If it will take a week, put the sticky-note that contains that task on the date one week before your mailing deadline.

Then go to the next step backwards - **"Board members write personal notes to those they know."** Discussion may include, "Well the last time, it took us a full week before all our board members came in to write their notes. So we'd best provide a week for that to happen." The sticky-note that says "Board member notes" will therefore be placed on the calendar one week before the stuffing and sealing.

And so on, until your final plan looks like the calendar shown here.

Final Calendared Plan

Deadlines and Flexibility:

One of the ultimate truths about planning is that "stuff happens." We're not talking about "planning stuff" here; we're talking about the other stuff of life. Likely as not, once you have created your implementation plan, something will happen to knock all those grand plans off kilter.

There are two approaches we recommend to accommodate the "stuff of life."

1) Plan for Reality.

Avoid planning based on the words, "If we had to get it out in only that amount of time, I guess we could..." Don't plan for what is possible under the very best of circumstances; plan for what is realistic.

Using the example of board members writing personal notes for the mailing, you may wish they would all come in on a particular day and just get those notes done. You might even say, "That should work just fine - they can all plan ahead. We'll give them plenty of notice."

In reality, though, board members are busy people, and you know even as you give them that date in advance that some will not be able to make it on that particular date.

So plan for reality, not for what "should" happen.

Planning Watchword: **No Shoulds**
Around our office, we have actually banished the word "should." Things either "are" or "are not." We have come to realize that "should" is usually little more than the wishful acknowledgment that what we had counted on happening isn't happening after all. Just ask any computer tech who tells you, "But it should work..."

2) Be Flexible.
One of the reasons we like using calendars with sticky notes is that things can be moved. Using sticky notes for planning is a way of acknowledging that sometimes stuff just happens over which we have no control.

Planning Watchword: **That's why God made sticky notes!**
With sticky notes, if an emergency arises, benchmarks can be adjusted, assignments can be re-allocated, and the work ultimately will get done. And we can be as forgiving and flexible as those notes are!

Don't Forget the Follow-Up
As you determine your steps - remember that the final step in any plan is really the follow-up. Incorporating the follow-up into your calendar makes it all part of that single effort, allowing you to be better assured that critical follow-up will happen.

For this particular effort, then, the following might be additional steps to calendar:

- Recipients receive the letter
- We receive responses to the letter
- Thank you notes to those who responded to the letter

To calendar these items, we might note that folks typically begin responding from the moment they receive our annual letter - and that it is likely they will receive the letter 2 days after it is sent. So we can place the sticky note that says "Recipients receive letter" 2 days after our mailing deadline.

Then, 2 days from the time they receive our letter, we might receive their response. (Sticky note added to the calendar for 2 days later).

Then, because it is our policy to follow up within 48 hours of receiving a response, we can calendar that we will perhaps be spending much of that next week sending thank you notes, as those responses come in.

4: Providing Assignments

The last step is to determine who will actually perform all those tasks. The simplest way to assign each task is to add the name of the person to whom that task has been assigned, right on each sticky note on the calendar.

If the project is complex, however, you may want to color code the sticky-notes - the green for Maria, the yellow for Steve, and so on. This makes it easy to see at a glance that if the calendar is filled with green, Maria is going to be spending a lot of her time on this project! (This is another time for perhaps moving those sticky notes around. Once you realize that all those tasks will be performed by one person, on top of all her other work, you can more realistically plan that what "should" have taken 2 weeks will really take 4 weeks or more!)

Step 8: Monitoring Your Plan

Monitoring is at the heart of both accountability and effectiveness.

If the staff doesn't monitor their own progress, they cannot know if they are getting the job done. And if the board doesn't monitor the whole organization's progress, they cannot lead or govern; all they can do is second-guess.

There are 2 basic steps in monitoring your plan:

1) Pre-Determine What You Will Measure

The first step in monitoring is to pre-determine what success will look like and how you will measure that. For a simple activity like a mailing, it may be rate of return, or some other easy-to-quantify measurement of success.

However, the more complex your goals and activities, the more the board will want to spend time in discussion to determine how they will measure success. Let's say one of your activities is as follows:

- Create a panel of community members who can help develop and guide our programs

Your board will want to spend time asking, "What exactly do we want the panel to achieve? And how will we know if they have achieved it?"

There is no right or wrong answer. You may decide that the mere formation of the group would be a success in its first year. Or you may decide that success would be defined by the group being actively engaged in making the programs the best they can be.

Regardless of what you want that effort to achieve, it is important to next discuss how you might measure your success. How will you know if that objective has been reached?

These are energizing discussions, as they get to the heart of what your organization is all about. How will we know if we are doing a good job at engaging the community? How can we measure the impact we are having in our community? You may find you enjoy those discussions so much, you will want to schedule time at each board meeting to discuss a portion of those issues!

2) Monitor Your Progress

Once you have determined what you want to measure, the whole effort is a waste of time if you fail to actually do the measuring.

The following is a simple example of a monitoring approach.

At each board meeting, the board will receive a report that monitors progress on the benchmarks of your plan. The report will answer:

Did we do what we said we would do by this date?

If so, was that effort successful?

If we did NOT do what we said we would do, why not? Do adjustments need to be made to the plan?

We recommend using a chart for this purpose, a sample of which is on the following pages. By recreating that chart in your word-processing program, updates can easily be made for each board meeting. The chart will have 3 columns:

★ The activities

★ The benchmark dates, along with what should be accomplished by that date (and by whom)

★ The status

When the period covered by your plan is completed, it is easy to monitor your success at achieving your goals if you have pre-determined what success will look like.

As you can see from the sample on page 67, there are some activities that are clearly on their way to not meeting their goals. With this report going to the board at every meeting, the board can make course corrections throughout the year, rather than looking back after a full year and wondering why the goal was not met.

Community Engagement Plan Monitoring Report

Date of Report: _____

Activities / Goals	Benchmarks & Dates	Status / Notes
Activity:	1)	1)
	2)	2)
	3)	3)
Goal:	4)	4)
Activity:	1)	1)
	2)	2)
	3)	3)
Goal:	4)	4)
Activity:	1)	1)
	2)	2)
	3)	3)
Goal:	4)	4)

Community Engagement Plan
Monitoring Report

Date of Report: February 15th

Activities / Goals	Benchmarks & Dates	Status / Notes
Activity: Public Speaking Campaign **Goal:** 1 speaking gig per month	1) Determine possible venues by January 31 2) Make contact with those venues, schedule gigs starting April 1 3) Create speaker kit by February 28 4) Speakers trained by March 15th	1) List completed 2) We have gigs scheduled for April, June and September! Working on others. 3) Speaker kit completed early! 4) Speaker training scheduled: March 10 - 6 people signed up.
Activity: Breakfast Campaign **Goal:** 6 breakfasts per board member per year	1) Board members create list of possible breakfast companions by November 30 2) Schedule breakfasts (ongoing) 3) Quarterly monitoring per board member of how many breakfasts they have done	1) Completed 2) Board has been slow to get started. 3) Jim has done 2 meetings, but none of the rest of the board has done any yet.
Activity: Volunteer Event **Goal:** 100 attendees - date set for spring cleaning	1) Planning committee established by September 15th 2) Committee complete workplan by October 31, and set date of event 3) Additional benchmarks will be added to monitoring report from the committee's plan	1) Completed 2) Date set for May 1. Committee says plan is done, but has not shared it with the board. 3) Committee has not submitted their workplan so we can change this report!

<u>Step 9:</u> Follow Up

Every once in a while something happens in our individual lives that makes us thankful for the incredible people who make that life worth living. Sometimes it is a catastrophe - a time when our friends are truly there for us. Sometimes it is when someone passes away, and we realize how limited our time is here on earth, and that none of us knows when our time is next.

It is at those times when we tend to look at the list of people we love being with, yet somehow don't manage to ever see. We vow to make time for those people, to call old friends, to spend time re-connecting. We go to lunch, have folks over for dinner, and as we spend that evening laughing and reminiscing, we vow to never again let so much time go by.

And then time goes by.

Life happens. We get busy. And we look up again, at the next crossroad, and we wonder, "How have I let so much time pass? Life is so fragile..."

Well, the same holds true for our organizations. The difference is that when we let relationships lapse on behalf of our organizations and our missions, it is not just two people who suffer - it is the whole community.

Follow-Up

The most important step in your whole plan will therefore be what you will do to make sure those relationships - those friendships - are nurtured on an ongoing basis. If we are talking about true 2-way engagement, this is not a one-shot deal. This is potentially a match between your passion and their passion - forever.

There are a number of ways to ensure follow-up occurs. Here are just a few ideas:

Build it Into the Plan

As you create your Community Engagement Plan, create one plan for that initial engagement: How will you meet and engage new friends for your organization? And then create a separate plan for follow-up, to ensure ongoing relationships with the people who are already engaged.

How often will you contact folks after that initial introduction? What form will that contact take, to ensure the relationship remains 2-way, and not just "sending out our newsletter?" That plan for ongoing engagement will be key to making sure the community remains engaged in your mission.

Create a Committee

Depending on the work required for following up with your Ongoing Engagement Plan, you may want to consider forming a Community Engagement Committee. This committee can do everything from sending thank you notes to making phone calls, from running volunteer and focus group events to making sure board members write personal notes on mailings.

And if you are thinking, "We already have too much work for our board and staff to do! One more committee will kill us!", then think again. Because there is no better way to keep folks engaged than to have non-board / non-staff volunteers involved in the very act of engaging the community. As you expand your army of supporters, put them to work ensuring that ever-growing army remains engaged with your work and your mission.

Make Follow-Up the Policy

There are various policies that can relate to follow-up. Here are just a few, specifically related to follow-up regarding gifts:

- Thank Before You Bank: No donations may be deposited into the bank until thank you notes or calls are made.
- 48 Hour Thank You: Thank you calls or notes must be completed within 48 hours of receipt of a gift.
- Board Thank-a-thons: Board members are required to spend X hours per year thanking supporters for their efforts - either in writing or by phone.

By creating policies, boards can then enforce that policy (yes, we are back to monitoring!). ED Evaluations can require documentation that friends have been followed up with in a timely manner. Board member letters of commitment (and evaluations) can require time spent in connecting or following up with friends.

One of the worst things that can happen to your organization is to lose a friend. Do your very best to maintain those friendships, and the community will be a far more engaged place.

Community Engagement Plan from Start to Finish

Community Engagement Plan from Start to Finish

In this section, you will find an illustrative example of a full plan, from start to finish. We will begin by sharing a bit about the organization. We will discuss the background behind the particular goal of the particular plan the organization is addressing. We will move through the steps, to show how the organization will determine who to engage, and then how they will prioritize and determine which of their various ideas to put into practice.

From there, you will see the thought process in creating the implementation plan. And you will further see how that thought process can require a bit of fluidity, as new ideas are folded into the plan, requiring adjustments along the way.

A Word About This Specific Illustration

For the examples used in the steps throughout this kit, we have emphasized engaging all sorts of people - individual donors, foundation officials, organizations with similar missions, as well as those who fall outside your immediate radar (local university professors, policy makers), and others.

We have also addressed all sorts of reasons one may want to engage those individuals, as we addressed the various goals of the various plans our organizations create.

In this illustration, however, we have chosen to focus on a specific goal, and a specific group of people to engage. And we have chosen both the goal and the people because of their critical importance to the work our organizations do.

Who This Illustration Engages

Our organizations often overlook the most critical group we could possibly engage - the everyday people who make up our communities. While we seek the advice of perceived industry experts and others whom we respect, the regular folks who make up our communities are all too frequently not on that list.

Here are just some of the reasons it is critical to engage "just people":

- When we engage regular, everyday community members, we are engaging the very people who will benefit from our services (either directly or indirectly).

- When we engage these members of our communities, we receive the benefit of their wisdom, caring, experience and passion - gifts that are otherwise squandered if left ignored.

- When we engage ordinary community members, we are engaging individuals who are living and breathing the very issues we care about, sometimes intensely so.

- And when we engage the regular, everyday members of our communities, we are laying the groundwork for building an army of advocacy and support for the causes we collectively care about.

The slogan has rung throughout the Disability Community says it most clearly: "Nothing about us without us" - in other words, "Don't decide things about us, without including us in that process!" The work that is most effective is work that is inclusive of both the folks who will be participating directly in your programs, and the community at large who will benefit from the program's very existence.

The Issue to be Addressed in this Ilustration

And that brings us to the issue itself. The example you will see on the following pages revolves around the issue of Program Diversity and Inclusion. For years, issues of Diversity and Inclusion have vexed many organizations. What we have come to learn through our own focus on creating cooperative, inclusive communities, is that the issue of Diversity is in large part a function of that bigger issue of Community Engagement. Towards that end, after this section, we have included a brief analysis of the Diversity Issue, from that Community Engagement perspective.

> **Note:** Because this Action Kit is integrally tied to the concepts and strategies in **FriendRaising**, the discussion of activities / strategies in Steps 3, 4 and 5 of this example will be more clearly understood if you review those strategies as you go. We have therefore provided the strategy numbers as they are listed in **FriendRaising**, for your ease in reviewing that material.

Example: Community Engagement Plan from Start to Finish*

Organization: Regional Theater Company
Our example is one of the most successful regional theater companies in the country, with a large established audience and a stable financial base.

Plan: Community Impact Plan

Vision: Our vision is a community that is always developing and encouraging the creative potential in all its citizens, and where the theater is one of many places where the community can come together to celebrate our humanity.

We will be able to best bring this vision to reality if our work is of interest to, and is seen by and appreciated by the largest percentage of the population.

Goal: Determine why our audience does not reflect the demographics of our community and how we can make our work more inclusive.

In a community with a diverse ethnic mix, where people classified as "white" comprise only 50% of the population, our audience is overwhelmingly white.

Community Engagement Goal: Determine what parts of our work we need to re-think to have this theater company truly represent the region - both in the plays we produce and the audiences who experience those plays.

Step 1:
Focus on the Community's Potential

In every subsequent step of the plan, we will engage within the context of our vision - that theater be an avenue towards developing and encouraging the creative potential in all residents of our community.

* This sample shows the Community Engagement Plan for only one of the organization's goals. Your plan will include all these steps for **each and every** goal of your plan.

Step 2:
How could Community Engagement help further our "Diversity" goal?

- By asking members of the major ethnic groups in our community for their wisdom, we can know what questions we should be asking and get their assistance in determining possible answers.

- By asking other successful theater groups around the country how they have addressed this issue, we can learn from them, and they can learn from us.

Step 3:
Who to engage?

Category: Hispanic Chamber of Commerce
Individuals: ED - Carlos Hernandez
(Can he help generate folks for us to talk with?)

Category: African American Chamber of Commerce
Individuals: ED - Ana Lewis
(Can she help generate folks for us to talk with?)

Category: Native American Chamber of Commerce
Individuals: ED - John Wilcox
(Can he help generate folks for us to talk with?)

Category: Asian American Chamber of Commerce
Individuals: ED - Ron Chu
(Can he help generate folks for us to talk with?)

Category: Our Board Members and Volunteers, and their Friends:
Individuals: For Board Members / Volunteers from all ethnic backgrounds, use the Life List Generator to determine who they know, who may also fit those categories

Category: Our current ticket holders
(To identify ticket holders to participate: We could announce at performances that we are seeking help, stationing volunteers in the lobby during intermission if they want to sign up. We could include an insert in the Playbill. We could do a mailing to our season ticket holders.)

Individuals: Those who are themselves Latino, African American, Native American or Asian American: Would they help us answer questions? Would they connect us with folks they know, who can also help?
Individuals: Those who are not in the targeted ethnic groups: Would they connect us with folks they know, who can help?

Category: Other successful Regional Theater Groups:

Individuals: Managing Directors of top 10 theater companies in the country

Step 4:
Strategies for Engaging People We Know

Chambers of Commerce Leaders:
Community Sleuthing (*Strategy #10 in FriendRaising*)

Breakfast campaign (*Strategy #9 in FriendRaising*)

Board members / Volunteers and their Friends:
Community Sleuthing (*Strategy #10 in FriendRaising*)

Breakfast campaign (*Strategy #9 in FriendRaising*)

Volunteer event (*Strategy #21-23 in FriendRaising*)

Interactive coffees (*Strategy #12 in FriendRaising*)

Individual Ticket Holders:
Community Sleuthing (*Strategy #10 in FriendRaising*)

Volunteer event (*Strategy #21-23 in FriendRaising*)

Interactive coffees (*Strategy #12 in FriendRaising*)

Regional Theater Managing Directors:
Community Sleuthing (*Strategy #10 in FriendRaising*)

Teleconferenced focus group (*Strategy #24 in FriendRaising*)

Step 5:
Strategies for Engaging People We DO NOT Know

In addition to the strategies above, where people we know will have introduced us to people we do not already know, the following are ways we could bring even more people to the table.

Chambers of Commerce (and perhaps other groups, such as Church groups, clubs, schools)

Speaking gigs

Generate other leads:

Write an article for newspaper asking for people to come forward and reply to our questions

Talk shows on local TV

Step 6:
Prioritizing

The Magic Matrix on page 83 was used to determine which activities to pursue.

From that matrix, the theater leaders chose to use only those activities that ranked above 75% of the total 30 possible points. That meant the group's first cut eliminated any activity ranked below 22. That focused the group on the following as possible strategies:
- Community Sleuthing Campaign
- Focus Groups
- Interactive Coffees
- Volunteer Event

The group then decided that the most important condition for this effort to be successful is the ability for the people they engage to share their wisdom. They therefore chose to include only those activities that ranked a "3" in the category of "Opportunity to Share Wisdom." That narrowed the group's choices to:
- Community Sleuthing Campaign
- Focus Groups
- Interactive Coffees

In their discussion of Focus Groups, the group got excited about the ability to teleconference several Managing Directors for a Focus Group. This would provide a way to move the whole group forward at once, about an issue they had each been privately considering from a professional standpoint for a long time.

When the discussion moved to holding Focus Groups in their own community, however, the group decided that it might make more sense to instead use the less formal environment of the Interactive Coffees. They felt that using the formal setting of a Focus Group to discuss such a sensitive issue might not work for community members who live and work together on a daily basis, and that the less formal Interactive Coffees might generate more frank and honest discussion. As they talked further about the Coffees, the group determined they would generate those Coffees through their Sleuthing activities, identifying possible hosts through those one-on-one discussions.

Therefore, their plan was shaping up to look like this:

For individuals in their community: Pursue Community Sleuthing and Interactive Coffees

For Managing Directors of other theater companies: Pursue individual phone sleuthing, plus a Focus Group via teleconference

Step 7:
Implementation Planning

In creating the plan, the Board had directed that the Managing Director convene a committee comprised of Staff, Board Members and community volunteers to spearhead this effort. They further directed that the committee provide progress reports every 60 days, with final recommendations in 6 months. The Board assigned primary responsibility for this effort to the Managing Director.

Brainstorming all the small steps that would have to take place for this effort to succeed, and then working backwards from the final report as the end goal, to determine what would have to happen, and in what order, the group assembled the following path to bring their plan to fruition:

Priority   **Activity**

12 → Analysis of responses provided to the board with recommendations (6 months of Sleuthing and Coffees)

11 → Hold the Managing Directors teleconferenced Focus Group: After the first few months of Sleuthing and Coffees, Managing Director will feel comfortable using those combined approaches to facilitate a Focus Group of other Managing Directors

10 → Interim reports every 2 months re: Results of Sleuthing and Coffees

9 → Ongoing: Group leaders will help facilitate Interactive Coffees

8 → Meet re: Interactive Coffees
   • Meeting: Develop script, brainstorm materials to provide
   • Determine who will lead these Coffees

7 → Sleuthing begins - setting appointments, having meetings, following up

6 → Sleuthing training

5 → Meetings to develop sleuthing training (including creating sleuthing questions)
   Ongoing: Add to list of sleuths
          Add to list of people to be sleuthed
          Recruit sleuths

4 → Begin recruiting sleuths

3 → First meeting of Program Diversity Committee
      Develop initial list of people to be sleuthed (note who their contact will be)
      Brainstorm possible sleuths

2 → Invite committee members to first meeting

1 → Brainstorm who should be on the Sleuthing Committee

Community Engagement Plan: From Start to Finish

When the group calendared the plan, it looked like this:

☑ February 9th   Brainstorm who will be on the Committee

☑ February 9th-13th   Invite committee members to the first meeting

☑ March 1st   First committee meeting
- Develop initial list of people to be sleuthed (note who their contact will be)
- Brainstorm possible sleuths

☑ March 2nd   Begin recruiting Sleuths!

☑ Ongoing
- Add to the list of Sleuths
  - Recruit Sleuths
  - Add to the list of people to be sleuthed

☑ March 8th   Develop training program for our Sleuths
- Allow 2-3 meetings to complete the creation of the program
- Create Sleuthing Questions as part of the training

☑ March 14th   2nd meeting to develop Sleuthing Training

☑ March 22nd   If needed, 3rd meeting to develop training

☑ April 5th   Sleuthing Training!

☑ April 6th   Sleuthing Begins!

☑ May 1st   Meet re: Interactive Coffees (to be hosted by those who are sleuthed, who are interested in helping and introducing their friends)

☑ June 1st   First interim report to Board

☑ By July 1st   Managing Director to have hosted / facilitated focus group of other Managing Directors

☑ August 1st   2nd interim report to Board

☑ October 1st   Analysis and recommendations to the Board

The group acknowledged that assignments would be made at the initial meeting, and then adjusted along the way.

Step 8:
Monitoring Progress

To monitor the progress of this effort, benchmark events were pulled from the Implementation Calendar. The group's monitoring report is on page 84.

Step 9:
Follow-Up

As the group considered what sorts of follow-up would be appropriate, the project began to gel further. The following are the additional activities they determined would help ensure the project's success, by ensuring the ongoing connection with the people they engage. As the effort proceeds, the group will further adjust and add their ideas and thoughts, to make the project more complete:

- For the duration of the Engagement effort, send a letter every quarter to anyone who has participated, specifically following up with the progress of the effort - with a personal note by the board member or ED or whomever was the conduit for bringing that person in.

- After the Board's 6 month review of the findings, have a "Town Hall Meeting" to reveal those findings to all participants in the effort, and to the public at large

- From that Town Hall Meeting (and additionally by invitation to anyone we have spoken with), invite interested individuals to form an advisory panel whose role will be to work with the staff to develop an approach that can accomplish the goals.

- 6 months from formation of panel, slate of recommendations to the Board, for final approval

The group felt this was the best way to engage the largest number of people as is practical, while still having concrete steps happening within approximately one year.

The group asked the Board to approve those changes in the plan, and they changed their Monitoring Report accordingly. The Implementation Calendar on page 81 shows that further thinking:

☑ February 9th   Brainstorm who will be on the Committee

☑ February 9th-13th Invite committee members to the first meeting

☑ March 1st   First committee meeting
- Develop initial list of people to be sleuthed (note who their contact will be)
- Brainstorm possible sleuths

☑ March 2nd   Begin recruiting Sleuths!
☑ Ongoing
- Add to the list of Sleuths
- Recruit Sleuths
- Add to the list of people to be sleuthed

☑ March 8th   Develop training program for our Sleuths
- Allow 2-3 meetings to complete the creation of the program
- Create Sleuthing Questions as part of the training

☑ March 14th   2nd meeting to develop Sleuthing Training

☑ March 22nd   If needed, 3rd meeting to develop training

☑ April 5th   Sleuthing Training!

☑ April 6th   Sleuthing Begins!

☑ May 1st   Meet re: Interactive Coffees (to be hosted by those who are sleuthed, who are interested in helping and introducing their friends)

☑ June 1st   First interim report to Board

☑ By July 1st   Managing Director to have hosted / facilitated focus group of other Managing Directors

📌 ADDED ☑ July 1st   Send Quarterly letter to those who have been contacted, to share findings to date and any other observations

☑ August 1st   2nd interim report to Board

📌 ADDED ☑ September 1st   Send Quarterly letter to those who have been contacted, to share findings to date and any other observations

☑ October 1st   Analysis and recommendations to the Board

📌 ADDED ☑ November 1st   "Town hall meeting" to reveal the findings of the engagement activities to participants in the effort, and to the public at large
- From that meeting (and by invitation to everyone the group has spoken with), form advisory panel (including staff) to develop an approach that can accomplish the goals.

📌 ADDED ☑ December 1st   First post-Town-Hall Advisory Panel Meeting
📌 ADDED ☑ April 1st   Deliver recommendations of Advisory Panel to Board for approval

Sample Plan: Results

As you can see from the Community Engagement activities for just this one goal, this single Community Engagement effort might have the following possible ripples:

- Deeper inclusion and broader diversity of audience, improving our program's impact in the community (the stated goal)

- Opportunities for great publicity

- Opportunities for learning all sorts of things that might be incorporated into the development of the program, that weren't part of the initial goal

- Opportunities for finding potential board members and other volunteers

- Opportunities for finding potential donors, partners, sponsors

- Opportunities we cannot even foretell (That's half the fun of Community Engagement!)

- What additional opportunities do you imagine could result from this effort?

   _____

   _____

   _____

Magic Matrix™ for Community Engagement

Strategies	1) How many engaged friends might this effort raise? (1=Few 3=Many)	2) How quickly will this effort raise? (1=Will take time 3=Immediately)	3) How much time will this new friend feel connected? (1=Will take time 3=Immediately)	4) How much cash investment will this effort need? (1=VERY 3=Low cash needs)	5) Could this effort accomplish more than one of our goals at once? (1=NO 3=YES)	6) Will this effort create a path to ongoing relationship, or is this really just an ask? (1=Just an ask 3=Builds relationships)	7) Can this effort be executed immediately or will it require prep time/planning? (1=Will take time 3=Immediately)	8) How much opportunity does this effort give our prospective friend(s) to share their wisdom? (1=No shared wisdom 3=Shares wisdom)	9) Will this activity create competition with others doing similar work? (1=YES 3=NO)	10) How dependent is this effort on decisions made by others? (1=Others will make decision 3=You make decision)	TOTAL
Speaking Campaign	3	1	3	2	3	3	2	1	2	1	21
Write for local paper	2	1	3	2	3	3	3	1	2	1	21
Local TV shows	2	1	3	3	3	3	2	1	2	1	21
Sleuthing Campaign	2 *Get two new names each time*	3	3	3	3	3	3	3	3	3	29
Focus Groups	3	3	3	2	3	3	2	3	3	3	28
Interactive Coffees	3	3	3	2 *Assist/Setup*	3	3	2	3	3	2	27
Volunteer Event	3	2	*Food/Postage, Invitations, Photos*	1	3	3	1	2	3	3	22

Community Engagement Plan
Monitoring Report

Date of Report: _____

Activities / Goals	Benchmarks & Dates
Activity: Community Sleuthing **Goal:** Speak with at least 50 individuals in 6 months (Including other Managing Directors)	1) March 1 - Committee meeting 2) April 5 - Sleuthing Training 3) June 1 - First interim report to Board 4) July 1 - Quarterly letter to those who were contacted 5) August 1 - 2nd interim report to Board 6) Sept 1 - Quarterly letter to those who were contacted 7) October 1 - Analysis and Recommendations to Board 8) November 1 - Town Hall Meeting 9) Dec 1 - First post-Town Hall Advisory Panel Meeting 10) April 1 - Final recommendations of Panel to Board
Activity: Interactive Coffees **Goal:** Host at least a dozen Coffees	1) May 1 - Meet to plan Interactive Coffees 2) June 1 - Begin hosting Coffees 3) June 1 - Include results in interim report to Board 4) July 1 - Quarterly letter to those who were contacted 5) August 1 - Include results in interim report to Board 6) Sept 1 - Quarterly letter to those who were contacted 7) Fold rest of plan into Sleuthing Plan
Activity: Focus Group Teleconference for Managing Directors **Goal:** Host 1 or 2 sessions, for maximum participation / attendance	1) July 1 - Conference Call Focus Group(s) completed 2) July 1 - Quarterly letter to those who were contacted 3) August 1 - Include results in interim report to Board 4) Sept 1 - Quarterly letter to those who were contacted 5) Fold rest of plan into Sleuthing Plan

PART 3

Community Engagement and Your Organization: Analysis & Application

ANALYSIS:

What Makes Community Engagement So Effective?

ANALYSIS: What Makes Community Engagement So Effective?

For five years, my business partner, Dimitri Petropolis, and I explored and experimented to find answers to the question, "What are the factors that create dramatic social change? What is going on when change happens, that is not happening in efforts that seem to create little to no change?"

In that exploration, we found six principles - what we have come to call *The Pollyanna Principles* - that are all present when dramatic community improvement and social change are occurring.

In the process of that research and experimentation, we found that when only some of the principles are embedded in a group's work, some positive change would occur, but that change was typically incremental rather than dramatic.

And when none of the principles were present in a group's work, we saw little to no visible change in the community the group served.

The six principles seem to be common sense... until we begin to see that work in the community benefit sector rarely incorporates more than one or two of the principles, when it incorporates any of them at all.

The Pollyanna Principles

The Ends:
- #1   We accomplish what we hold ourselves accountable for.
- #2   Each and every one of us is creating the future, every day, whether we do so consciously or not.

The Means:
- #3   Everyone and everything is interconnected and interdependent, whether we acknowledge that or not.
- #4   "Being the change we want to see" means walking the talk of our values.
- #5   Strength builds upon our strengths, not our weaknesses.
- #6   Individuals will go where systems lead them

Analysis: The Pollyanna Principles and Community Engagement

Pollyanna Principle #6 notes that people will go where systems lead them. Seen through the lens of the Pollyanna Principles, it becomes clear why systems rooted in Community Engagement are so dramatically more effective than the current norm in Community Benefit work.

Pollyanna Principle #1:
We accomplish what we hold ourselves accountable for.

Pollyanna Principle #2:
Each and every one of us is creating the future, every day, whether we do so consciously or not.

If anything is evident in the stories and how-to steps in this Action Kit, it is that Community Engagement extends accountability beyond just the four walls of an organization. If we want our whole community to become a force for change, with each and every member of our community holding him/herself accountable for creating a better future, the two-way exchange of Community Engagement accomplishes that.

This became infinitely clear through the stories on pages 20 - 26.

When we built the Diaper Bank in Phoenix, we started out knowing almost no one. But fifty people wound up working for months on end to make the Phoenix Diaper Bank a reality. By engaging those individuals in what was possible for their community, they held themselves accountable for accomplishing that.

When the doctors assisting the Cancer Support Group were engaged in real dialogue, those doctors began holding themselves accountable. Their formation of an advisory group is evidence of that heightened sense of responsibility for making a difference.

There is no better example of a group holding itself accountable for the difference it intended to make in its community than Every Voice in Action's Youth Crew. First, the young people themselves are being taught how they can hold themselves accountable and act upon that accountability, to create community change. Secondly, though, the foundation is eschewing the top-down, "we-know-best" philanthropy of days past, in favor of a truly engaged philanthropy, working with the population they serve, and creating end results no single one of those parties could have achieved on their own.

Community Engagement transforms "people who care" into people who are holding themselves accountable, taking ownership of the issues a program is addressing. That is what it means to build an engaged community.

With Community Engagement, then, the means do not merely align behind the future a group wishes to create for its community. The means - building an engaged community - are themselves part of that vision for the future!

Pollyanna Principle #3:
Everyone and everything is interconnected and interdependent, whether we acknowledge that or not.

Pollyanna Principle #4:
"Being the change we want to see" means walking the talk of our values.

Pollyanna Principle #5:
Strength builds upon our strengths, not our weaknesses.

In our initial Community Engagement work to build the Diaper Bank in Phoenix, one comment seemed to arise, almost verbatim, in virtually every one of those meetings: "What you are suggesting may work in Tucson. But Tucson is smaller, more cohesive. The organizations in Phoenix simply will not work together."

This comment occurred in almost every meeting we had, regardless of whether we were meeting with business people or funders or agency representatives themselves. It got to the point where my partner, Dimitri, and I had to stifle laughter when someone mentioned this "fact," as we had begun placing bets on how long it might take before we would hear those words!

The facts, however, consistently contradicted this assumption. Given the opportunity to engage themselves in an effort that often required long hours of meetings as well as a hefty dose of physical labor - physically handling hundreds of thousands of diapers - the people who built the Valley Diaper Bank took on those tasks joyfully.

Why joyfully? Because working together on something a whole group cares about feels good. The higher spirit in us humans craves those connections. When our work is aligned with the flow of our interconnectedness, we tap into the spirit that is already there, waiting for us to bring it out. That sense of something bigger than each of us becomes yet another strength upon which to build. What was formerly a "chore" becomes a task met with enthusiasm.

The flip side of connectedness and cooperation is competition. In Phoenix, the representatives of 50 organizations who were often positioned as competitors built the Diaper Bank together. During that process, they shared what might otherwise have been considered "trade secrets." They shared data.

They even shared diapers! One participant announced that they had just received a donation of far more Size 3 diapers than they could use. Did anyone need the remainder?

Engagement turns us all into partners, chipping in together to make a difference. It requires that we walk a talk of shared values, modeling the behaviors we hope to inspire in others, as that is the only way the end result will come to pass. Every Voice in Action is the most obvious example of what it looks like when an effort is walking its talk through engagement. However, the truth is all these efforts put higher values into practice than we often see in traditional "nonprofit" work. Each of them was being the change they wanted to see in their communities.

It is a lot easier to insulate ourselves from walking our talk when we are not connecting in a meaningful way with those who might point out our inconsistencies. The more honestly we are engaging with the community we serve, learning and working with them side by side, the more we can build upon the values we all share, to create the future we all want.

Community Engagement is therefore a system that leverages the sense of connection / commitment to something we all care about, building individual strength, organizational strength, and community strength all at the same time. In the end, that spirit of interconnectedness and cooperation not only feels terrific; it is the only practical, vision-based road to turning our communities' highest aspirations into reality.

~~~~~~~~~~~~~~~~~~~~~~~~~~~~~~~~~~~~~~

Considering the Pollyanna Principles as you re-read the questions and forms in this Action Kit, you begin to see why Community Engagement is such a powerful way of approaching your organization's work. In the end, we realize it's about moving beyond "being *the change* we want to see."

When we deeply engage in all our work, we are actually "being *the community* we want to see." We are modeling the behaviors we want to see in others, showing them what is possible by the simple act of the way we do our work.

ANALYSIS:

Community Engagement vs. Traditional Marketing and Outreach

ANALYSIS: Community Engagement vs. Traditional Marketing and Outreach

Open the workshop catalog of any Nonprofit Resource Center, and you will find a class on Marketing. The blurb likely says something about using business tools to make your organization strong - competing for scarce resources, or differentiating yourself from others doing similar work.

When Dimitri and I first begin speaking about Community Engagement with a group, they often ask if this isn't just another form of marketing (or, as it is commonly called in Community Benefit work, "outreach.").

While this Action Kit highlights so many of the multiple benefits of having your organization be more engaged at the core, the following chart clarifies just some of the critical differences between Community Engagement and traditional marketing.

Community Engagement	Marketing
Goal: Efforts aim at community strength. Side-benefit: Individual programs gain strength through shared, collective efforts.	**Goal:** Efforts aim at individual organizational strength.
Rooted in cooperation. Sees other organizations as partners towards creating a healthy, vibrant community. Creates a cooperative spirit of "all of us together."	**Rooted in competition.** Sees other organizations as enemies in the battle for scarce resources. Creates a competitive spirit of "us and them."
Asks: "What can we accomplish together, that none of us can accomplish on our own?"	**Asks:** "How will we differentiate our organization from others doing similar work, so supporters give to us?" (Not always explicitly stated, but always implicitly present: "...and not to those others")
Two way conversation. Authentically exchanging knowledge and ideas.	**One way message.** Based on positioning - telling people what we believe will encourage them to do what we want them to do.
Rooted in feelings of collective strength and confidence.	**Rooted in** feelings of individual survival - fear and weakness.
When taught in workshops, formerly "competing" organizations begin building bonds right there in the workshop. Teaching engagement builds and perpetuates community.	**When taught in workshops**, participants keep to themselves, seeing their learning and thinking as proprietary. Teaching marketing builds and perpetuates individual siloed organizations.

Groups have the best chance of creating healthy, vibrant communities when they link arms together as one interconnected, interdependent force for good. And that leads to one more observation about marketing and community engagement:

> When groups engage communities in building solutions together, there is no need for marketing and outreach and going "out to the community." Because those participants are already there, building it and running it and supporting it with you.

And so, it is our hope that one of these days, instead of finding Marketing classes at Nonprofit Resource Centers, we will see only courses on Community Engagement, leaving "marketing" where it belongs - selling candy bars and cars.

Community Engagement and Board Diversity

Community Engagement and Board Diversity

Following on the heels of the Program Diversity example in the last section, we would be remiss if we did not take a moment to focus on the issue of Board Diversity and its direct relationship to Community Engagement.

Board Diversity is one of the hottest topics in the sector. Just about every organization knows the need for a diverse board, regardless of why they think Diversity is important. Sometimes the motivation is that board members realize the board's make-up does not reflect the community - whether the issue is race or age or socio-economic status or etc. - and they sincerely understand the value such inclusion would add to their decision-making. Sometimes the discussion is prompted instead by a funder, who is questioning the make-up of the board.

Regardless of their motivation, once this topic is raised with a board, the progression often follows the same pattern:
- The board airs the frustrations the group has faced in trying to add "diversity" to the board.
- The board brainstorms a list of names of "people of color" (for example) whom they might approach, typically people they know from work, or from Rotary or other professional networking settings.
- Those individuals are approached, and almost all of them respond that they are already over-committed. (Typically this is because those individuals are the same names on the lists of every other board in town that is seeking diversity!)
- At the next board meeting, board members report the following: "I spoke with Joan and Becca and Joshua, as we had discussed. And they all like our organization, but they are all over-committed. I just have no idea where else to look."

If this cycle sounds familiar - if issues related to diversity and inclusion have been a problem for your board - you will find that Community Engagement is the most effective way to put this issue to rest once and for all.

"Board Diversity" as a Symptom
While the issue of Board Diversity is serious, that issue is not the real problem. A lack of board diversity is merely a symptom.

> There is a direct correlation between board diversity (and staff diversity and volunteer diversity) and the level of engagement the organization has with the community it serves. The less inclusive the board (or the staff / volunteers), the more likely it is that the organization also has a low level of direct engagement with the community it serves.

Therefore, the seemingly ironic solution to the "Board Diversity Issue" is to stop focusing on finding "diverse" board members! The solution is to instead start engaging the community.

When you begin to deeply engage your community in the work you do - as happened with the Regional Theater Company illustration in the previous section - those "Board Diversity" symptoms (and staff / volunteer diversity and program inclusion and etc.) begin to take care of themselves.

Working With vs. Working For
Let's go back to the definition for Community Engagement that we presented on page 13 of this kit:
> Community Engagement is the process of building relationships with community members who will work ***side-by-side*** with you as an ***ongoing partner***, in any and every way imaginable, building an army of support for your mission, with the ***end goal*** of making the community a better place to live.

Community members and organization representatives working side-by-side.

Community members as ongoing partners.

All of us sharing the same end goal.

Is that how your programs are built? If yours are like most programs, the answer is "no." Most programs - whether they are in the field of the arts, economic development, human services, or other facets of the Community Benefit world - most programs are still built upon the Charitable Model that developed in days of old.

The Charitable Model is one in which benevolent benefactors who wanted to help those in need (or wanted to support struggling yet talented artists) chose the means through which they would provide that assistance, based on the assumption that they, as the benefactors, knew what was best.

The Charitable Model could be described as follows:
> **We, the experts, provide this service for you, the recipients.**

Regardless of the Community Benefit arena (arts, human services, etc.), the Charitable Model has become the most common approach to delivering service in this sector. We do our work ***"for"*** our communities.

Community Engagement turns that approach on its ear. Instead of working ***"for"*** the community, Community Engagement is about working ***"with"*** the community.

Here is the difference:

Working FOR the Community:

An organization that is working FOR the community does its program planning in-house, with staff, perhaps the board, perhaps some community professionals, perhaps some volunteers, and perhaps - if the organization is forward-thinking - some recipients of the service.

This primarily internal group determines what service is needed, and determines what that program should look like, perhaps including in their work a survey or focus group of participants and/or community members.

This internal group then executes the plans for making that service happen.

When the program is up and running, the organization may survey existing users of the service, perhaps also surveying those not using the service, to see why they are not using it. The survey is typically written by the organization's staff, with little or no community input into the development of those questions.

Those survey respondents, plus the few community members who were included in that initial planning process comprise the full extent of the involvement of the community in creating its own service.

Working WITH the Community:

An organization that is working WITH the community acts as the facilitator of community members, pulling the program out of the individual and collective knowledge and wisdom of those community members.

The program may be implemented by the organization, but it is created through the participation of the community that will use the program, all aimed at making that program as effective as possible for their population(s). The example in the previous section illustrates what it means to work WITH the community to develop programs.

Working *for* the community was indeed the history of our sector. And after all these years, breaking those habits requires practice.

- Working *with* the community requires new skills - Community Engagement skills. And new skills become second nature only with practice.
- It will also require practice because working *with* the community will take the staff and the board outside their comfort zone, whether that is the comfort zone of doing work the way they've learned to do it, or the more disquieting comfort zone issue of having to interact as equals with folks who we may perceive to be different from us.

- Lastly, it will require practice because working **with** the community can be perceived as giving up control.

Regardless of why we choose not to engage the community directly in our work, it becomes clear that "diversity issues" are a direct result of that lack of inclusion, connection, engagement at all levels of the organization. If the diverse communities our organizations target with their services were deeply involved in making our programs the most effective they could be, it would be unlikely that "board diversity" would be the issue it has become. It would be far more likely those individuals would already be there - not because they are Hispanic or gay or Muslim or elderly, but because they are a caring part of the community, and they are already involved.

From this discussion, you can also see that "diversity" is about far more than race - it is about whatever it means to fully represent the community you serve. It may have to do with ethnic background or religion. It may have to do with age. Or sexual preference. Or income level. Or gender. It may have to do with a particular disability. If instead of the word "diversity", we talked about "Community Engagement in creating the most effective programs possible," we would know instinctively the best way to accomplish that - simply ask for participation from the very populations who will use our programs, whoever they may be.

The most critical issue, therefore, isn't that symptom - lack of board diversity. The most critical issue is that your programs cannot provide the maximum benefit to your community without your community's direct involvement in those programs.

Which brings us back to Community Engagement. And it further brings us back to the point we have made repeatedly, throughout this kit - that through Community Engagement we can accomplish so much more than simply "engaging supporters so they will donate more money."

When you have community members who are deeply engaged with bringing your mission to life in their community, diversity is no longer a problem, and support is no longer a problem. With an engaged community, you will be able to accomplish far more than you dreamed possible, because you are all working together - side by side, as ongoing partners - to make the community a better place to live.

Community Engagement and Sustainability

Community Engagement and Sustainability

One of the most critical components to creating impact in your community is the ability to assure community members that they will be able to count on your efforts - not just today, but tomorrow, and thousands of tomorrows after that. That assurance is the very definition of sustainability - reliability and dependability for the services your community counts on and the change they want you to help create.

Having read to this point in this Action Kit, you are already seeing that integrating and engaging your community in your work and your dreams is a big piece of sustaining that work and those dreams.

In the Community Benefit sector, though, when folks talk about "sustainability," they tend to focus on "financial sustainability." Just mention the word "sustainability" in a room full of leaders in this sector, and you will hear all about the latest fundraising fads. It seems someone always has some panacea or another - the "individual donor movement" or the "entrepreneurial" movement, and so on.

The problem with all those approaches is that they focus first and foremost on "competing for the money." And as you've read elsewhere in this Action Kit, if anything will preclude groups from creating significant community impact, it is categorizing our most powerful potential allies as "the enemy!"

When organizations start focusing on sustainability beyond just money, though, an amazing thing happens. They find they are not only able to create more impact in their communities, they actually become more sustainable as individual organizations in the process.

The following steps show how programs can be developed to simultaneously build community strength and organizational strength for the long haul.

Sustainability Step 1: Start Where We All Agree

As we have stressed throughout this Action Kit, if we are to build strong efforts to benefit our communities - the reason our organizations exist in the first place - it is important to first look beyond our organizations and out towards that community. There are multiple reasons for this, as you will see in the other steps. But the most important reason is that in reality, few people care about your organization nearly as much as they care about their community.

So Step 1 is to identify what the REAL goal is. And that real goal is that your community be better in some way, and hopefully significantly better.

Consider "Community Success" through the eyes of a food bank.

- Is your definition of success "a community where everyone who needs food has access to the food bank?"
- Or would success be a community where everyone who needs food has access to food, period?
- Or might you define even larger success, perhaps a community where everyone has all their basic needs met?
- Or dreaming even bigger, might you see success as a community that is a healthy, resilient, humane place for everyone to live?

Virtually everyone can agree upon those higher goals. Is there anyone in your community who does not want your community to be healthy? So Step 1 is to identify what part of that vision for community success your work will aim to achieve.

Sustainability Step 2: Engage!

Looking at the goals of your mission, whether you are building a new program, revamping an existing program, or considering how to sustain your mission overall, you already have a sense that engagement is the starting point. And when the context for each of the goals about which you are engaging is the powerful vision of a healthy, vibrant community, you will be connecting with people at the level of their greatest aspirations. You can't get much more engaging than that!

Sustainability Step 3: Sharing Resources

In other books and workshops I teach, I often compare the strength of a program to the strength of a well-built and well-maintained house. Just as a strong house needs strong infrastructure, so does a strong program. The strongest program infrastructure is one that tightly interweaves resources from all across your community, building engaged strength into the very skeleton of your program.

A single thread, standing on its own, can be blown away by the slightest breeze. But it would take quite a wind to blow away a tightly interwoven blanket of many threads. When we build the infrastructure of our programs by interweaving the resources of others in our communities, we are building a foundation that is resilient, that cannot be easily dismantled when times get tough.

The example of the Diaper Bank on pages 21 & 22 begins to show what that interwoven infrastructure can look like.

So how does one build a program upon that infrastructure of shared responsibility? First map out your program, starting from the very first step - perhaps the moment someone calls on the phone or the moment someone walks in the door. What happens first? Then what? Then what?

For every one of those functions, ask, "Is someone in town already doing that function? And if so, can we partner with them?"

If one of those functions is the need for transportation to get people to your program, is someone in town already transporting people, and might you partner with them? If you need storage space, does another organization have excess space you might be able to use? If you need bookkeeping, is someone in town already doing bookkeeping, with whom you might be able to partner?

Going back through the steps in this Action Kit, you will quickly be able to identify people and organizations to engage for each function.

The infrastructure strength that comes from building your programs on a base of shared resources is more than the obvious - that it will likely cost less to build your program. The real strength comes from the strength of that interwoven fabric. By building your programs upon the community's existing resources, every one of those partners feels ownership of your program in a way that builds engagement directly into the core of your program. Just look at what it did for the Diaper Bank!

By building programs upon a base of shared resources, we are therefore building strong engaged programs while simultaneously building community strength. We are doing nothing less than building a spirit of cooperation and engagement in our communities through the simple act of building a single program.

And that interwoven, integrated, cooperatively built program cannot help but be more sustainable than the stand-alone, independent programs we so commonly see.

Community Engagement and Your Board

Community Engagement and Your Board

One of the most common questions about Community Engagement has to do with the role of the Board in engagement activities.

And as it is with all things related to boards, the answer can be found in the organizational chart.

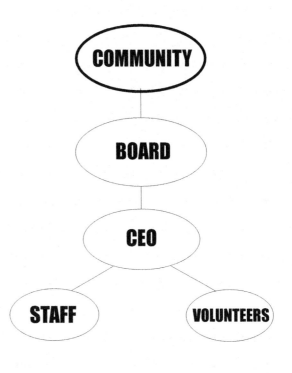

The Board has a unique place in the org chart. The Board sits in the top box when it comes to the organization. But as volunteer community members, the Board is also the direct link to the community.

It is from that dual position that we can easily determine the role of the Board when it comes to Community Engagement.

1) From its internal position at the top of the organizational chart, the Board governs the organization.
2) From its position as the link to the community, however, the Board represents the organization to the community, and the community to the organization.

Boards spend most of their education hours focused on that first role - the internal role as leaders of the organization. Boards spend very little time, however, learning about the critically important role of "ambassador" - the link to the community.

The Board's Ambassadorial Role

Acting as ambassadors, Board Members are a big part of the organization's Community Engagement efforts. To date, that has been taken to mean that Boards should be involved in fundraising. However, Board Members often break into hives at the mere suggestion that they should ask their friends for money.

Fortunately, "asking for money" is not what Community Engagement is all about. As a result, almost all board members feel comfortable performing their Ambassadorial role.

Community Engagement is a simple thing. It is rooted in celebrating all the various gifts every person has to share, just as we do with our personal friends. When it comes to our friends, we overlook their faults, because they make us laugh; because they invite us over for pizza when we've had a bad day; because they think our kids are adorable (or understand when they're being not-so-adorable). We celebrate what is good in our friends, what is precious in them.

And that is how Board Members will make friends for your organization. They will get to know people, tapping into one of the most specials gifts each of us has to share - the desire to make our communities better places to live.

How do we do that? We ask them to become part of our circle, however they fit. We talk to them about our mission, and we ask for their thoughts about that mission - their ideas, their wisdom, their life experience. We share our stories, and we ask them to share theirs. And we celebrate the connections we find between their experience and our mission.*

Making it Policy
Some boards choose to turn their Ambassadorial Role into policy. As part of their letter of commitment, board members are required to introduce X new friends to the organization each year. Depending on the board, it could be one per month or one per year. The point is that it is made clear up front, the moment the new board member sees that letter of commitment, that engaging the community is a big part of what it means to be on the board.

Community Engagement for Boards - Many Rewards in One
Board members who participate in these kinds of Community Engagement activities become directly engaged with the mission in a way that has everything to do with effective leadership and governance.

Acting as the organization's ambassadors, Board Members who actively engage the community become more deeply engaged with the organization.

The rewards of community engagement for boards therefore become more and more obvious, the more engaged those board members become:

Community Engagement work is fun.

It is energizing for board members, for the organization as a whole, and for the community members you engage.

It builds sustainability for the community and for your work.

And importantly, Community Engagement build strength into your board. Because an engaged board is not only making a difference for your organization and your community; they are engaging others to do the same.

*For 100 Community Engagement strategies your Board can not only do, but enjoy, see **FriendRaising: Community Engagement Strategies for Boards Who Hate Fundraising But Love Making Friends**

About the Author

Hildy Gottlieb is co-founder of Creating the Future, a living laboratory dedicated to finding the most effective methods for organizations to create a healthy, vibrant, humane future for our world.

Hildy has been called "the most innovative and practical thinker in our sector." Her book, *The Pollyanna Principles: Reinventing "Nonprofit Organizations" to Create the Future of Our World*, details her groundbreaking approach to aiming the work of the Community Benefit Sector at its highest potential - creating the future of our world.

A prolific writer and advocate for the sector's potential and a consultant to community organizations since 1993, Hildy helped develop the current Masters degree program in Community Leadership at Duquesne University, where she and her partner, Dimitri Petropolis, have taught as professors. Hildy's workbooks have all become industry standards and are used as texts in both undergraduate and graduate programs around the world.

Among Hildy's prior accomplishments, she developed the Family Home Gardening Program at Pio Decimo Center in Tucson, to ensure low income family had fresh produce, by teaching them to grow that produce themselves.

And most notably, she and Dimitri co-founded the world's first Diaper Bank, as well as the Diaper Banking movement in the U.S.

Hildy's numerous awards include a Points of Light Citation from President Bill Clinton. Her writing has been seen in publications throughout the community benefit sector, including the Chronicle of Philanthropy, where she currently hosts the monthly podcast interview program, Making Change - interviewing change leaders from around the world.

When not working, Hildy can be found in the garden, at the movies, shooting photos, or watching the Daily Show.